A Girl Named Maria

A Girl Named Maria

✦

The Story of an Adoption; The Death of a Child

Valerie S Kreutzer

iUniverse, Inc.
New York   Bloomington

A Girl Named Maria

The Story of an Adoption; The Death of a Child

iUniverse books may be ordered through booksellers or by contacting:

iUniverse
1663 Liberty Drive
Bloomington, IN 47403
www.iuniverse.com
1-800-Authors (1-800-288-4677)

ISBN: 978-0-595-49705-8 (pbk)
ISBN: 978-0-595-61217-8 (ebk)

iUniverse Rev Date 12/08/2008
Printed in the United States of America

iUniverse rev. date: 12/15/2008

Like with a fallen tree, we appreciate the full length of a life only after it has ended.

—Anne Morrow Lindbergh

For now we see through a glass, darkly; but then face to face: Now I know in part; but then shall I know even as also I am known.

—1. Corinthians 13:12 (King James Version)

Contents

INTRODUCTION

When I adopted two-year-old Maria Consuelo Mendez in Bogota, Colombia, I was convinced that love can conquer all. Our early years of blissful bonding in Washington DC seemed to prove me right. But during her teens, Maria's severe learning disability, a stubborn streak, and her impulsive behavior contrived to challenge me to the core. Desperate, I sought advice from books, experts, and support groups. I learned that many adoptive parents are equally perplexed by their child's hidden handicaps, struggles over identity, and misdirected rages.

When Maria died at twenty-one, the diary she left behind revealed a deep yearning and desperate search for her birth family. As I reviewed her legacy, it dawned on me that our mother-daughter story of conflict, survival, and reconciliation may resonate with other parents who raise an adopted child.

Though born into misery, Maria died happy and in love. Many who knew her were touched by her exuberance and also by her struggles. "To all who have helped me in this life, I say thanks," she wrote in her high school graduation yearbook. This narrative mentions many of these good people— family, friends, neighbors, teachers, advisors, and therapists. I changed the names of friends and acquaintances to protect their privacy but kept the names of members in our extended family.

Throughout the writing of this book, Maria's portrait leaned against my computer. "Tell it like it was," she whispered as I chronicled the yin-yang patterns of her sojourn. Maria was my muse.

1.

DEATHS AND A FUNERAL

The first call came at 2:00 a.m. It woke me, but I ignored it. Four rings and then silence. I knew the answering machine would kick in. I looked at the clock and told myself to go back to sleep. Someone, no doubt, had dialed the wrong number.

The next call came at 2:30 a.m. It had an insistent ring. I stiffened in my fetal pose. I should get up and answer, I thought. But I couldn't move, now full of foreboding. Twenty minutes later there was an urgent, loud knock on my door—I couldn't ignore it. Peeking through the viewer, I saw two men dressed in black.

"What do you want?" I asked.

"This is the police. We need to talk to you."

"Wait, I need to get dressed."

I grabbed the gray-and-white-checkered bathrobe Maria had given me that Christmas of her senior year. I pulled the belt tightly and opened the door just a crack.

"Do you have a daughter Maria in Florida?" one man asked.

"Yes."

"May I come in?" I let go of the door and retreated toward the coat closet. In the dim light from the living room, his tall, dark frame loomed large.

"I hope it isn't bad news," I mumbled limply.

"Yes, it is bad news." He paused. "She is dead."

"No," I protested.

"Yes," he said firmly.

1

I felt faint as blood drained toward my shaking legs. "Please sit down," he urged, gesturing toward the sofa. Shocked beyond comprehension, I obeyed. He then proceeded to tell me that a car carrying Maria, her boyfriend David, and another young man had crashed into a tree in the curve of a rural road in Ocala, Florida. There were no witnesses. The accident had happened at ten o'clock that night. It had taken the rescue team an hour to retrieve the bodies from the wreck; they were pronounced dead on arrival at the hospital.

"Here is a number you can call," said the officer, handing me a piece of paper. "Is there someone you can call to be with you?" he asked. I shook my head. I was pretty new in Seattle, and didn't feel I could rouse anyone with such devastating news. "You know," said the young man who looked Hispanic, "I've done this for sixteen years and it's always different and never easy."

"You look a little like her," I said, reaching for his hand. He nodded. I wanted him to stay but he seemed anxious to exit the scene before my shocked numbness gave way to raw emotion.

After he left, I sought the warmth of my gas fireplace. Something made me want to spread my arms like wings. And as I did, I saw Maria clearly on my left. Her face was serious, composed, beautiful. Looking down as if onto the crash, I heard her say: "It's okay. It's okay. It's okay."

"How amazing," said David's father a few days later when we met in Florida for the first time. "I've had a similar experience. I was driving a day after the accident and I saw David clearly in the windshield. 'Don't worry, Dad,' he said. 'I'm okay.' I thought I was hallucinating. But now that you tell me about your experience, I believe our children are trying to tell us something."

Ever since the night of November 15, 2000, I have been obsessed with trying to understand the short life and sudden death of my adopted daughter, Maria Consuelo. She left me with an abundance of memories and pieces of an unfinished puzzle.

During the last months of her life, Maria had lived with David, whom she had met playing pool in a popular bar in Ocala, Florida. During an hour-long phone call shortly before her death, she had told me in great detail about meeting and falling in love with David—tall, blond, and very handsome. Their flirtation started with casual glances, a few smiles, a couple of drinks, and a dance at a party.

Her name was Maria Consuelo Kreutzer Mendez Benkarani, she told him, and, good-naturedly, David would call her sometimes by the whole string of her names. She had been born in Colombia, South America, and was adopted by Valerie, who was German, she told him. She had lived most of her life in Washington DC. At eighteen she had married Simo Benkarani, a Moroccan with an expired student visa, and a year later had left him after his run-ins with the law. She had come with a new boyfriend to Florida, but that relationship had quickly soured.

Adopted? She was adopted? Well, so was he, David informed her. And besides, his roots were also German. Maria laughed. She had lived at war with her German mom and now she was falling in love with a man whose blond hair and fair complexion would easily fit into the German landscape.

David, only a year older than Maria, had also been married and had a son. When his wife gave birth to a second son while David served in the army, David contested paternity and got a divorce. The army had given him an honorable discharge. "Once you've straightened out your personal affairs, you can come back," his officer had told him. Inclined to drift without ambitions and direction, David had done well in the military and hoped to rejoin.

Maria was amazed at his story because she was in the process of applying to the National Guard in her latest attempt to find a place and structure in her chaotic twenty-one-year-old life. But the application process had come to a halt when she couldn't provide proof of citizenship. During her year of itinerant living, she had lost her U.S. passport and naturalization documents. Replacing them would take time. Meanwhile, she was staying with Joe, who had offered his living room couch. But cohabitation with Joe turned ugly whenever he got drunk and demanded sexual favors.

On the night of their fatal attraction, Maria had come with Joe to the bar. Seeing him get drunk, she dreaded returning to his apartment. "Would you stay and play billiards with me?" she asked David. "Gladly," he said. And so they pointed their chalked cues at plastic balls in friendly competition. With a steady clack-clack, their yellow, purple, and orange balls smacked against each other before disappearing with a thud into the black hole. She had a good eye, a natural stroke, and a fluid motion that knocked him over. Once out, David conceded, grinning, "Okay, Maria Consuelo Kreutzer Mendez Benkarani, you won." In billiards and most other games, Maria was a winner.

They kept playing and talking, and soon it became clear that she had no place to go. That's when David offered shelter at his little house that sat behind his parents' red farmhouse in Silver Springs. "But I'm not a one-night girl," she cautioned. "Don't worry, I'm not that kind of guy either," he assured her. "But, if you prefer, you can stay at my parents' house. My mom wouldn't mind," he said. And so she went home with David because he felt safe.

Three days later, David urged his mother, Natasha, to meet Maria, "because she is too scared to leave the house." When they met, Natasha's heart went out to this girl who had arrived on her doorstep with nothing but the clothes on her body. She took Maria grocery shopping and bought her Marlboros, gave her a change of clothes, and gradually fell in love with Maria, just as her David had. Maria came to call Natasha "Nan."

"Nan thinks that I'm the best girl David has ever had," Maria reported to me over the phone. "And you know what?" she added with a giggle, "Nan was a professional wrestler and still gets fan mail—and I get to answer it because Nan has arthritis and can hardly write."

Sometimes, when David was away, Maria crawled into bed with Natasha. They watched wrestling matches and had heart-to-heart talks. Maria had been angry at her mom, she confessed. Had written her a letter saying that she didn't want to hear from her again, and hadn't seen her in almost two years. "Because I blamed her for all the things that went wrong in my life. But now I'm finished with kicking the dog," she told Natasha, who encouraged Maria to rendezvous with me. Not at Thanksgiving, because Natasha wanted Maria at a family gathering in Georgia, but perhaps in January, for Maria's twenty-second birthday?

"How would you like to meet me at the end of January in Washington DC?" Maria asked during our last phone conversation. She sounded so excited about life with David and her new job at the hardware store.

"We're real busy at the store because the hunting season is about to begin," she informed me with an air of self-importance.

"Yes, I'd love to meet you in DC," I said. "And we'll celebrate with all our friends, the way we always did!"

I was thrilled.

Ten days later Maria was dead.

Maria and David

Natasha had told me that the minister who would preside at the funeral for our children was a family friend. He was in his eighties, deaf, and a Baptist, she said. "I hope he's not going to preach fire and brimstone," I mumbled to my sister Claudia, who accompanied me on this journey.

We met with the minister at the funeral parlor the day before. I asked to see him alone. We found a small room and sat facing each other. I sobbed and poured out my motherly pain, my despair over this cruel end to an unfinished relationship, regrets over opportunities missed, the guilt of survival, the burden of having to continue life without my child.

Never mind that he was deaf. I needed a wailing wall for my grief. But the old man seemed to listen. He had learned to read lips, he explained, and his soothing words let me know that he knew grief in all shapes and sizes, including mine. He had a serious heart condition and would be dying soon. "The Lord may call me any time, and I am ready," he said. Though wrapped in my veil of sorrow, I could sense his serenity.

But what really endeared the old man to me was the little apology that preceded his eulogy the next day. "I may not be able to pronounce the young lady's name correctly," he said. "I asked a Spanish teacher at my church, and she practiced with me, but, since I can't hear, I may not have learned it right." And then he proved his point by calling her "Consulu."

After that, he avoided names altogether, talked about "this young woman and this young man," and gave us the general gist of Baptist theology on death and resurrection. Sitting on a wooden folding chair between Claudia and Natasha, I tuned out. I looked past the green tent and the coffins with their towering bouquets of red roses. We were in a quiet oasis at the end of a dirt road. It was a family cemetery, sparsely populated with gravestones and markers. The limbs of scrawny trees were covered with Spanish moss, whose lose ends were swaying in the breezes.

"Will you bring her body home?" Natasha had asked on the telephone on the night of the accident. "Home," I had wondered. "Maria has never been to Seattle and I'm still new here, trying to make it my home. I don't know what to do." That's when she offered a space next to David in her family's cemetery in Zephyrhills. "We'd be honored," Natasha had said, offering to make the arrangements.

My attention returned to the eulogy just as the minister pointed to David's coffin, saying, "And this young lady led this young man (pointing to Maria's coffin) back to the Lord." Some gigantic mix-up, no doubt! Not only was the old man confused about the identity of the coffins, but surely my Maria, raised on Unitarian principles, had not led her boyfriend "back to the Lord." "What was that all about?" I asked Natasha after the last Amen.

"Well," she said, quietly weeping, "David had belonged to a cult and Maria had gotten him to quit the group. We were just getting ready to all go to church on Sundays." *Maybe*, I thought. As for this cult business, David's former buddies still seemed to count him in. During the reception at the funeral parlor, a group of young men and women, tattooed and pierced, clad in black leather with dangling silver chains, had clanked in to pay their respects. They had wanted to place mementos into David's open coffin, but his father had stopped them. And when they had marched to the funeral at the cemetery, I saw David's father meet them halfway. After a little talk, they made a U-turn, leaving us to the Christian ritual.

David's older brother started to sing "Amazing Grace" and, when he broke down, his wife, who seemed to know all scripture references by heart, stood up and helped him get through:

When we've been there ten thousand years, bright shining as the sun,
We've no less days to sing God's praise than when we'd first begun.

My sister read a prayer she had found in Maria's diary: "I thank you, God, for the stars, moon, sun, earth, a roof over my head, a bed to sleep in, food to eat, money to spend, items to enjoy," Maria had written a year earlier at Thanksgiving. "I thank you for my health and the health of the ones I care about, including friends and family. I thank you for the strength to face each day. I thank you for the ability to face each situation. I only wish to find peace and happiness in life and love."

During the last four months of her life, Maria seemed to have found it. "David is the love of my life," she had confessed to Natasha, who in turn told her, "You're the best girl David has ever had." They lived happily in the little house behind David's parents' house. They were silly and playful. They also seriously contemplated a future together. "I know they were meant for each other," Natasha lamented. But in this life we were left to bed them into Florida's sandy soil.

"This concludes the service," the funeral director announced, expecting us to disperse. Claudia and I lingered. In our tradition, the sprinkling of earth over the lowered coffin is a loving gesture of farewell. At this funeral, however, technology took over. Two men and a crane started maneuvering monstrous vaults into the gaping holes. Next, they lowered the wooden caskets into the concrete liners, sealing them with lids that closed with a loud thud.

Claudia and I shook our heads. We were used to wooden caskets and bodies disintegrating into the soil, according to the laws of nature—earth to earth, ashes to ashes. "Maria will be the last person to rise from the dead," my sister joked grimly.

Once the vault lids were in place, I threw a handful of dirt on top of Maria's, and the vault echoed with a hollow sound. "I love you," I said, throwing another. And another, and yet another. I wanted to embrace the whole mound of earth and hurl myself into the hole. That's where I belonged. My sorrow was deeper than six feet.

2.

WHO WAS SHE?

For almost twenty years, Maria Consuelo was the center of my universe.

Our love affair began in Bogota, Columbia, where she had been found abandoned in the lavatory of a small downtown cafeteria. She was approximately fifteen months old and undernourished. The owner of the cafeteria later recalled seeing a young woman with the child. The woman wore a *ruana*, a blanket-like cloak, and had quickly disappeared.

The police who came to pick her up named her Maria Consuelo Mendez. They placed her picture with an SOS in *El Tiempo*, the largest Bogota daily. When nobody came to claim her, she was transferred to the orphanage of the state welfare agency, Bienestar.

After three months, Bienestar declared her adoptable. Out of the stack of applications from would-be parents in Europe and the United States, they pulled my folder. With a paper clip, our lives were joined for better or worse. To my mind, the mystery of this bureaucratic matchmaking rivals the miracle of any biological conception.

In October of 1980, Bienestar announced their decision in a five-line letter. They asked that I come to Bogota to take custody of the toddler. The four-year-long search for my daughter was about to end.

As I sat on the plane from Washington DC, memories of the agonizing process flashed through my mind: the phone calls and dozens of letters that had gone to agencies and individuals in Latin America and India ... the notes of rejection I had received ... the Salvadoran lawyer who had made false promises ... the American woman in India who had deceived me ... the stacks of validated, notarized, and authenticated documents that had been

9

sent out verifying my good health, stable employment, upright citizenship, and my genuine love for children …

On the plane I also remembered my first disastrous trip to Bogota, only nine months earlier. Having tried for years to find a child for adoption, I had been inspired to follow the lead of a State Department colleague who had just returned from Bogota with Jackie, a spunky four-year-old whose fearless dark eyes were framed by a mop of thick black hair.

"Why don't you activate your professional connections?" my colleague had suggested. That was easy since I worked for the U.S. Information Agency's (USIA) Latin American press service, and officers at our embassies knew my byline from almost daily reports and features. Within a few weeks, I sat in Public Affairs Officer Mike Kramer's office at the U.S. Embassy in Bogota.

Mike welcomed me warmly. A father and grandfather himself, he liked the purpose of my mission and was glad to lend a hand. He introduced me to Yolanda, a Puerto Rican woman who worked in the embassy's consular section and helped issue visas to Colombian children adopted by Americans. She handed me a list of orphanages with which she was in almost daily contact.

Next, Mike introduced me to a young summer intern in the embassy's public affairs section. Olga was bilingual, had cascading blond curls (*Are they for real?* I wondered) and a curvy body squeezed into a mini-outfit. She was chatty and soon let me know what was uppermost on her mind: whether or not to attend the Marines' Ball, an elegant annual affair organized by the young men who guarded the embassy. A friend of hers, Olga confided, had gone to the ball, and, having been swept off her feet, was now married to a U.S. Marine and lived in New York. I got the impression that escaping Colombia was a goal for many, as evidenced by the long line of visa applicants that curled around the embassy compound.

As I set out on my mission with Olga, a list of orphanages, and a chauffeur-driven car, I felt confident that I'd soon find my daughter. After all, I was offering a nurturing, stable home and many opportunities in the United States—destination of the huddled masses.

First we visited the Catholic orphanages. Their administrators were friendly but started to frown when I mentioned that I was single and not Catholic. It seemed that they had mile-long waiting lists of Catholic couples eager to adopt, and my quest didn't warrant consideration.

The early 1980s, as I was to learn, saw a shortage of adoptable babies in the United States. Several factors had contributed to this. One was the 1973 U.S. Supreme Court decision allowing abortions in the first trimester. Another was the widespread use of improved contraception. But the most important factor was the change in our attitude toward single-parent families and toward children born out of wedlock. Divorce had contributed to the fact that many children were now raised by single mothers. Social acceptance of this trend encouraged unwed mothers to keep their babies. In 1971, 90 percent of the babies born out of wedlock were put up for adoption. Ten years later, when I was searching, more than ninety percent of them were kept by their mothers. That's why those of us who wanted to adopt had to look elsewhere.

During my visits, I found that Colombia's orphanages were full of adorable children. They seemed to sense my purpose for being there and crowded around me, calling me "Mama-mama." But most of them, an administrator explained, still had a relative unwilling to release the child for adoption. In Colombia, as in many other poor countries without social security and old age pensions, children are the only insurance against the hardships of old age. And so, some distant uncle in Colombia's hills and jungles was banking on this kid who was hanging on my skirt. "I'd like to take you with me, but I can't," I whispered to a clinging toddler.

After several visits to Catholic institutions, I finally came to Bienestar, Colombia's health and human services department. The woman in charge of adoptions didn't even blink when I told her that I was single and over forty. "*No problema*," she said, citing Colombia's law that did not allow discrimination of adoptive parents on the basis of sex, marital status, age, religion, and nationality. I sighed with relief.

Now, as for two-year-old girls—my stated preference—there were few, she explained. Would I consider a baby? she asked. No, I said. Nightly feedings seemed incompatible with the demands of my inflexible work schedule. Two would be ideal, I thought, envisioning my healthy, happy daughter toddling off to day care while I covered congressional hearings, interviewed visiting politicians, and raced toward deadlines. All right, they'd keep me in mind, the woman promised vaguely, and Olga, the chauffeur, and I trekked back to the embassy empty-handed.

"Don't worry," said Yolanda, the visa queen, "I'll keep reminding my contacts on your behalf." As it turned out, she kept her word.

On my last day in Bogota, I treated myself to some sightseeing and ventured toward Mt. Serrate, the mountain that looms 8,860 feet over the city, promising a fabulous view. A funicular, Swiss-made and thus inspiring confidence (*Though, when was this rusty cable railway last inspected?*) took us to the top. "Awesome," I said to the man next to me, an American. He lived in Brazil, it turned out, and was attending a psychology symposium. At our feet spread the city of six million, surrounded by the hills of the Andes, forever green from daily mists and drizzles. The midday sun shone brightly on the tiled red roofs below us. We agreed to walk back to town and continue our interesting conversation.

And so we descended on the winding road past emerald mountains, quite charmed by our chance encounter, when suddenly a group of young men from nowhere rushed toward us. They grabbed my camera and shoulder bag and pinned my companion to the ground, systematically picking his pockets and removing his watch and shoes. We screamed and I pleaded with an older passing man to help us, but he just waved me away and kept walking. Once they had what they wanted, the young men scrambled up the steep slopes to little huts clinging to the hillside.

"At least return her passport," my shoeless companion yelled after them, and down came my U.S. passport, followed by my empty purse. A young girl ran to retrieve them, offering both with a pained expression that made me think she didn't approve of the assault. She could have been the robbers' little sister, but her sympathies were clearly with me. From the grass she picked a coin that had fallen out of the purse and held it up for me. "Keep it," I said, wishing I could give her more.

We tried to flag down passing cars, and, when one finally stopped several hundred feet below, we ran to catch it. The driver was anxious to get away. "You were lucky," he said. "You could have been killed."

I didn't feel lucky when I sat an hour later in Mike Kramer's office, telling him of my week of disappointments that had climaxed with highway robbery. As I dissolved into tears, Mike retrieved a box of Kleenex and gently tried to contradict my disappointment. With hundreds of homeless children living in Bogota's streets, and new cases of abandonment announced in the papers almost daily, there was a child waiting for me, he was sure. My best bet was to keep in touch with Yolanda, he suggested.

Over the next nine months, Yolanda was my lifeline. Whenever she talked to orphanage officials in the context of issuing a visa, she'd ask: "And what about a child for Valerie?" There was a cute three-year old, she reported. Great, I said. But the judge hadn't released her yet. Next there was one less than two. Wonderful, I said. Again, the courts didn't give their clearance. Finally, I received the letter from Bienestar, informing me of twenty-one-month-old Maria Consuelo Mendez. I should come immediately to take custody of the child, they wrote. The letter included a Polaroid of a forlorn girl in a pink dress with a pageboy haircut and a scar on her cheek.

I was beside myself with excitement. Grabbing note and photo, I jumped into my car and careened down the hill to my friend Katie, the mother of a one-year-old. Cars kept honking because I was oblivious to right-of-ways or traffic signs. My mind was focused on this sweet girl standing on a table, a lost little soul defenseless against the harsh flash of a camera. *I will make you feel safe and glad, and I will put balm on your scars,* I vowed, as I screeched to a halt in front of Katie's house. She shared my joy. "But you know," Katie said, "she looks older than two," confirming my first intuition.

At work I asked to take maternity leave for the adoption process. "Unheard of," said my boss. "Sure, go ahead," said my friendly department head. Off I went with a few quickly purchased items of clothing for my two-year-old.

Yolanda met me at the airport. She shared a house with her father, a retired ambassador, and had invited me to stay with her family for a few days. "Can I bring you anything?" I had asked. "Nothing for me," she said, "but could you bring my children some Christmas presents?" I did, and her daughter and three sons—from three previous marriages—happily unwrapped my gifts of T-shirts, toys, school and art supplies. Yolanda and her family had a live-in maid and middle-class comforts, but her children, unlike their U.S. counterparts, had a sparse wardrobe and few toys. They were unspoiled and cheerful, had imagination, and knew how to make something out of nothing. In preparation for Christmas, they had built a lovely nativity scene with moss and wooden figures in one corner of the living room.

On my second day in Bogota, I met my Colombian lawyer, to whom I had given power of attorney. He spoke no English, but my Spanish crash course had prepared me sufficiently to comprehend his outline of the legal process. Yes, Maria Consuelo Mendez had been released into my custody by the courts, my lawyer said, and on Monday, December 15, I would be able to pick her up at the Bienestar office.

"Tomorrow I will meet Maria Consuelo," I wrote in my diary. "I look at her picture all day and try to imagine what she is like. Tomorrow night I will be a mother—I can't believe it!"

Arriving at Bienestar at nine in the morning, I met a couple and their daughter from France, waiting to receive a two-year-old boy, a younger sibling for their adopted nine-year-old daughter. We chatted anxiously, and, every time the door opened, we froze mid-sentence. But it would just be a clerk dumping another set of manila folders on a desk.

It was after four in the afternoon when we heard wailing down the hall. First came the boy with a head of curls and a face void of expression. He easily moved from the social worker's arm into the enthusiastic embrace of his new mother. "What a gorgeous child, what a beautiful boy we have," the father kept exclaiming, as the older girl wrapped her arms around her mother.

Next came a wailing Maria Consuelo. Pearls of anguish hung from the longest eyelashes I had ever seen. Once more she was to be abandoned, and, with all the strength she could muster, she struggled against her fate. Sensing her pain and feeling my joy, I just cried along.

We tried to ease the transition by walking up and down the dimly lit corridor. "What is 'I love you' in Spanish?" I asked the social worker—my course at the Foreign Service Institute hadn't taught me that. I then repeated "*te quiero, te quiero*" like a mantra. She clung to her caregiver and raised her hands in tentative gestures of defiance. Her misery reminded me of an earlier scene of abandonment.

It was a bitter cold January in 1945, when I was seven and living in Schneidemuehl, Germany, now part of Poland. World War II was coming to an end, and the Russian front had moved close enough for us to hear its thunder. Like everyone else, we worried whether we'd get out alive. Miraculously, my father, a Methodist minister, had received permission to attend a conference in Berlin, eight hours away by train. My parents decided that he should take me, the youngest, with him. My mother and three sisters would try to follow, God willing.

Civilian travel had come to a virtual halt. Trains were transporting troops and ammunition to the front, returning with the wounded and half dead. The train station was clogged with refugees. Most of them were Ukrainians fleeing the onslaught of the Russian army.

Women in long skirts and kerchiefs sat on their bundles half dazed. One of them held out her little boy. The child was about two and was dressed in a brown hand-knit suit. His mother's soft plea was in Ukrainian, which we did not understand, but her language of desperation needed no translation.

I gripped my father's leather-gloved hand as we passed the peasant woman and her child. We still looked respectable, just having left our parish home. Within a few days, we too would be homeless and part of the colossal trek of starving, ragged refugees.

I never forgot the little boy in the brown suit. As a seven-year-old, I knew that my mother would never offer me to strangers. My trust in her was innate. For me, it was as it should be. In the Hebrew Bible, the archetypal bond between mother and child is often used to symbolize God's relationship with humans. "Can a woman forget her sucking child, that she should not have compassion on the son of her womb?" asks the Prophet Isaiah (Isaiah 49:15, King James Version). And, anticipating the miserable fate of the Maria Consuelos of this world, the prophet assures us: "Yea, they may forget, yet will I not forget thee." Divine assurance counters life's cruelties.

Returning from my flashback, I was again at Bienestar where it was five in the afternoon and everyone was itching to go home. Without further ado, the wailing Maria Consuelo was placed into my arms. As I received her, I promised the invisible woman who had birthed this child: I will love and cherish her. Until death do us part.

In the car on our way to Yolanda's house, Maria crouched on the floor at my feet, refusing to let me hold her. "*Mira, mira* [look, look]," cried my well-meaning lawyer, the father of two, as he dramatically manipulated the clutch in hopes of coaxing the child out of her misery. "*Te quiero, te quiero*," I kept saying, which means "I want you."

During the next few days I wondered whether I did. "She has a little diarrhea," the social worker had whispered when she handed me my daughter. "A little," I gasped when a deluge of shit enveloped me the first night we spent together in a single bed. I later learned, in the disinfected environs of Washington DC's Group Health, that her torrents were signs of amoebas, a rare tapeworm, and tropical viruses all wrapped into one big mud slide. The medicine to cure her had to be ordered from Atlanta's Center for Disease Control, and I had to sign all sorts of disclaimers in case of deadly side effects.

But that was weeks later. For now we were buying Pampers in bulk. We changed and washed the screaming child from top to toe at least four times a day and discovered that Bogota's sun wasn't strong enough to dry the many changes of her skimpy wardrobe.

Yolanda's resourceful children were a blessing. Maria stopped crying only when they crowded around. Twelve-year-old Eddie was especially adept at changing her diapers. And when nine-year-old Celina offered half her breakfast bun, Maria greedily also grabbed the other. She clutched the bread trembling with defiance. This child has known hunger and knows how to fight for survival, I realized.

She also had a head full of lice. We noticed them when we took her to get photos for the Colombian passport, a prerequisite for the coveted U.S. visa that would bring us home to Washington DC.

Between lice, a runny nose, and diarrhea I deciphered a hungry and traumatized child—my new daughter—who avoided eye contact and turned away from me to cry, cry, cry. Complete exhaustion soon cured any and all of my romantic notions of blissful motherhood. Ours was not a love at first sight. "*Te quiero*," I mumbled, wondering whether I did.

I had brought her a doll, thinking that she'd love playing with it as I once had. But the doll landed in a corner with a flourish of contempt. Stuffed animals were her thing—hundreds of them, we later discovered. For now, there were no toys, especially after we moved into an apartment my lawyer rented for his clients—adoptive parents from Europe and the United States. What were we to do all day while we waited for the passport and visa?

I ripped a newspaper into strips and crushed them into little balls that we piled into heaps, kicked around the room, or threw into the air, and for a little while Maria would be interested before collapsing again into her bottomless sorrow. She would push me away and crouch along the wall like a wounded animal in need of shelter. I crawled right behind her, and, when she was exhausted, she would let me scoop her into my arms as she fell asleep. During those little naps she sweated profusely, and awaking would rally her spirits to play a little, only to collapse again into sobs. On her third day, she woke from her nap with a first faint little smile of recognition. That was the turning point. I knew then that we'd make it.

She didn't talk, but understood and had a way of communicating without words. She made hissing sounds—"tsss, tsss, tsss"—and "talked" a lot that way. Buckling on her blue sandals, I said "*zapatos*," and she whispered the word with clear pronunciation—not exactly a baby's first word. Another time when we encountered a dog I said "*perro*," pointing, and she repeated "*perro*" right back. It made me think that she must have been verbal before she lost her speech during the trauma of abandonment.

I also noticed that she didn't care for women much and preferred men. Whenever my lawyer showed his face, she lit up. She really got excited when he came with a group of friends. I had to hold on to her, or she'd have gladly walked with them into the sunset.

Visiting the orphanage where she had stayed for the past six months, I tried to find out as much as I could. The director gave me a tour of the facility, introducing me as "*la mama de Maria Consuelo.*" "I want to get adopted too," said the seamstress who was sewing little blue frocks for the children. She was sitting next to the so-called infirmary, a bare room furnished only with three cribs. Maria had spent several weeks at a time there, usually with bronchitis. Once she had also been hospitalized with pneumonia, the records showed. The poor baby, I thought, fighting for her life without the comfort of a relative at her bedside!

And no wonder she had been sick so often! The orphanage, housed in an old *hacienda* a few miles out of town, was damp and smelled moldy even in the middle of the day when temperatures creep to fifty-eight degrees Fahrenheit. Since Bogota is close to the equator, the climate is the same year-round. Like most homes, the orphanage had no heat and the children survived the chilly nights under thin blankets.

There were a few babies lying in cribs. A curly-haired blond boy reminded me that Colombians are a mixed race of Indians, Europeans, and Africans, with looks ranging from blond and blue-eyed to black. In the dining hall, toddlers sat at long tables on little chairs with leather seats. I wondered whether the mush in their bowls was enough to still their hunger. Maria, I learned, had gotten the scar on her cheek from a food fight with a boy.

A young physician, who had just made his rounds, advised me on how to take care of Maria's "little diarrhea" with some rehydration formula. He obviously didn't have the tools to properly diagnose her intestinal turmoil.

The teachers produced a stack of Maria's pencil drawings showing promise and said that she was an excellent climber on the dilapidated jungle gym. She was known for her incessant wailing, and one young woman had ended up carrying her around all day. "Wawe, wawe, wawe," Maria kept lamenting. One teacher had visited the little cafeteria where Maria had been found, hoping to get some leads and more information on the child. But the owner simply shook his head and shrugged his shoulders. He vaguely remembered the young woman coming in with a child. Had she left the child at the cafeteria hoping that the girl would be found and fed? Or had she tried to get the child out of harm's way? Could a mother do that? Or was it a relative who had left her?

A decade later, when Maria became quite obsessed with the puzzle of her early years, she once told me that she had an image of her mother. "I am lying in a crib," she recalled, "and a very young woman stands with her back to the crib—I cannot see her. But I believe she is my mother."

And at another time, Maria told me an astounding vision of a man whom she believed to be her father. "I see him sitting at a table," she said. "A gun is lying on the table, with its registration number face down."

It is likely that Maria, born at the end of the 1970s, was surrounded by violence. Columbia has endured decades of brutal armed conflict between the national army, left-wing guerrillas, and right-wing paramilitaries, locked in a three-way struggle for power and drug money.

In her book *Death Beat*, the brave and brilliant Colombian journalist Maria Jimena Duzan writes that Colombia has been a country "where murder could be carried out with impunity, both before and after the rise of the drug traffickers; a country that lacked a tradition of tolerance for ideas opposed to one's own; a country where many politicians had been the main figures in scandals in their own departments, diverting public funds for their private uses."

In the countryside, the gaping rift between absentee landowners and landless and hungry peasants had been a breeding ground for violence long before drugs entered the scene. At a 1982 State Department seminar on Latin America, I watched a documentary on the plight of Colombia's peasant poor. The film focused on a typical family trying to live off the land. The crops from their small and barren acre were insufficient to feed a family, and the farmer, practically indentured to the landowner, earned too little to supplement his income. He would leave for the city, he explained, perhaps find more lucrative work there, and, once established, come back for his family. The emaciated farmer was surrounded by small children with extended bellies and blond hair—both signs of malnutrition. They could have been Maria Consuelo's siblings, I thought.

At the end of my two-week stay in Bogota, my lawyer handed me a ribbon-wrapped packet of sealed and stamped papers that would get us out of Colombia and into the United States. As we headed for the airport, Maria struggled with all her might against getting into the taxi, then threw herself kicking and screaming on the floor of the terminal. It was as if she knew that she was leaving her country and all that was familiar—the sounds, the smells, the faces, the language, the climate, and the landscape. It took every ounce of my might to wrap her into my arms while presenting the documents and dragging the diaper bag.

Perhaps she was afraid that I was just another person taking her somewhere to be handed over. But on the plane to Miami she began to relax, during immigration procedures she was almost cheerful, and, on the flight to Washington DC, she curled up with contentment, soon sleeping soundly. Arriving in DC to cooler temperatures just before Christmas, I wrapped her in my red sweater and headed for a taxi.

"I just adopted her in Colombia," I explained to the friendly African-American driver. "That's wonderful," he said, "welcome home!" And then turning, he patted her head lightly as if to bestow a blessing.

"We are home—Valerie and Maria Consuelo," I wrote on the door at our co-op. It didn't take long before our neighbors arrived like magi bearing essential gifts of Pampers, juice, and toys. They were moved by the sight of the little forlorn waif standing in the middle of my living room, and, kneeling down, they smiled "welcome" into her serious face.

Back in Bogota, when she had screamed under the shower—the only place where I could clean her from avalanches of diarrhea—I had dreamed of Maria soaking in the warm water of our tub. She'd have so much fun splashing around, I imagined. Instead, she gingerly moved her hands up and down, relishing the soothing warmth with a sense of awe, and I, sitting on the edge of the tub, felt in tune with her pleasure. That's what I had wanted from parenting, I realized, seeing the world anew through my child's eyes. As for happy splashing, it took at least a week before Maria caught on and soaked the floor.

Not all the firsts were wondrous. We went shoe shopping because those little blue sandals wouldn't do in wintry Washington. But Maria refused to accept the exchange. The new *zapatos* flew past the friendly sales clerk, and, making her point, Maria marched out of the store still wearing her Colombian sandals. Changes of any kind were difficult for her. She loved parties—the bigger the better—and would have a fit when we had to leave. It made me wonder if she had been born into a large family.

The worst experiences revolved around taking a bus, which was the best mode of transportation in our Adams Morgan neighborhood. She would refuse to get on the bus, and she would struggle with all her might once I had forced her on. I had to hold her in an iron grip and couldn't help that her protest and screaming made us the center of attention. Diligent bureaucrats would slowly fold up their copies of the *Washington Post* with sighs of exasperation. Squirming on my lap as if it were a matter of survival, she usually managed to kick off her beloved *zapatos*, one by one. When we got off, sympathetic passengers would hand me missing shoes with gestures of goodwill and good riddance. Once the bus trip was over, Maria would slump into her stroller, spent and content. I often chose to walk long distances to avoid wrestling matches on the bus. *Did buses perhaps drive her into abandonment?* I wondered.

Maria couldn't tell me, but she let me know that she needed to be with me, day and night. We were inseparable during the first weeks of our Washington life. We ate together, played together, and shopped together. She followed me into the bathroom, handed me the tissue, and she insisted on sleeping with me.

The latter concerned me because I had consulted baby guru Dr. Spock, who told me authoritatively that children need to sleep in their own beds. Period. And if they try to climb out of their cribs, put tennis netting over it, said the good doctor. But Maria didn't agree and followed me screaming when I tried to slip from her bedside after elaborate goodnight rituals. So, still believing in Dr. Spock, I put a sleeping bag and then a cot next to my bed, insisting on the spirit of the separation.

After attending a family workshop, I changed my policy and let her sleep with me. The workshop leader said it was most natural that children wanted to sleep with their parents and that most people got married primarily so they would have someone to sleep with. Converted by these new insights, I struck a bargain with my child: She'd start in her bed, and, if she should wake in the middle of the night, she could come and sleep with me. That gave me back my own nighttime habit of reading a few pages before falling asleep.

I soon could count on her appearing in my doorframe around eleven, lugging two bags, one with her stuffed animals, the other with clothes for the next day. She'd snuggle into the contours of my body and we'd sleep soundly. Good night, Dr. Spock!

Years later when Maria hurled "I hate you, and you are not my mother" into my anxious face, I almost forgot that we had once been inseparable. There was a time when she craved to crawl into me, as if wanting to be born again by me, her second mother. And yes, I would have gladly birthed her—my commitment was total.

And so was hers. When our dear friend Deborah announced that she was getting married to Robert, a fellow student at Antioch Law School, I shared the good news with Maria.

"What is married?" she asked.

"That's when two people who love each other promise to stay together for the rest of their lives."

Pause.

"Are we married?"

Maria was three and a half when our upstairs neighbor Judy gave birth to a boy and often came to visit. Maria was fascinated by Judy's breastfeeding of the baby. "Is that what you did with me?" she asked. "No, I didn't," I said, taking a deep breath, "because I adopted you." She seemed to accept my explanation. But, later that night, she climbed into my lap and touched my breast. "Would you like to try?" I asked, deciphering her longing. She nodded. I bared my breast and let her suckle. I was empty and explained why. It was a moment of profound intimacy that sealed the relationship of our early years.

Valerie and Maria "married"

3.

BIRTHDAYS

Maria's Colombian passport said that she was born January 24, 1979. She held on to that dark-green document to her dying day. To obtain it, we had to get photos at a little back-alley shop in Bogota. Maria screamed throughout the session, wouldn't sit by herself, and was frightened by the camera's old-fashioned flash. The passport shows a teary and miserable child of about two.

For years I wondered how she had obtained her birth date. I assume that some authority—perhaps a physician—determined her age during her six-month stay at the orphanage. There are scientific ways of determining age, but at Bienestar the process seemed to have been based on intuition. When I met Maria she was one month short of two, according to the made-up birth certificate. She had a set of perfect white teeth and well-developed motor skills. She talked only in tsss-tsss-tsss whispers, seemed to understand very well, but was still in diapers. By one, Colombian babies are usually potty trained, Yolanda informed me. She should know since she had raised four babies. Yolanda interviewed Maria on the subject, and Maria nodded yes, she always uses the potty—but then didn't. There were inconsistencies between some of Maria's skills and behaviors, we agreed.

To her credit, Maria was no shrinking violet. By wailing and fighting, she often succeeded in getting what she needed. I saved a news clipping showing my five-year-old in a summer camp in the Black Forest in Germany. In the story's photo, Maria sits smack in the center in the camp director's lap. The article mentions "*eine kleine Amerikanerin* [a little American girl]" who created havoc for lack of understanding German. Maria was oblivious to the problem, and it took my sister Heidi's skillful intervention to keep camp organizers from sending Maria home. Asked about her experience, *die kleine Amerikanerin* said that she had a great time at camp, thank you.

Maria knew how to assert herself. And, while she often pushed me to the brink of exhaustion, I was also glad for her brave efforts to prevail. A decade after our first encounter in Bogota, I observed first-hand the blessing of adopting a kicking and screaming child.

In the spring of 1990, I was on a business trip in Romania. Nicolae Ceaucescu's communist dictatorship had crumbled only a few months before. Part of his cruel legacy were thousands of children warehoused in orphanages because Ceaucescu had not permitted birth control, and starving mothers had deposited their babies in orphanages where they lingered in their cribs with little human contact. As soon as the images of these abandoned children became known in the United States, prospective parents eagerly lined up to adopt. Among the passengers on my flight from Bucharest to Vienna were off-duty flight attendants who had volunteered for baby lifts. One young woman carried a baby in a basket and had a toddler draped to her back. "Now we're getting on the plane for the ride home," the woman whispered. "Your mom and dad are already waiting for you." The children couldn't understand her, of course, but her cooing voice sounded soothing. The baby and toddler, however, never responded. They did not utter a sound and barely moved.

Later I read news accounts about the horrendous difficulties adoptive parents encountered while trying to coax these little shutdown Romanians back to life. Thank goodness, I often thought, Maria still knew her feelings. She didn't transition without protest into her new mother's arms.

The day before I met Maria, I had spent a few hours with a social worker at Bienestar to finalize adoption papers. The woman was very upset over an adoption that had gone awry. A six-year-old girl had refused to be adopted by a French woman, she told me. The girl had spent a few days with the social worker's family that included a new baby. When told that she would be sent off with the single French woman who barely spoke Spanish, the girl had thrown a tantrum and refused to go. She wanted to stay with a family that included a baby, she demanded. "The adoption is off," cried the social worker. "The woman is returning to France empty-handed, and the girl will go back to the orphanage and may never have another chance to be adopted." Maria didn't have a say in her adoption. If she had been older, would she have come with me? I often wondered.

But back to the question of Maria's birth date. While there was uncertainty about her age, Maria totally embraced January 24 as her birthday. Christmas was barely over when all talk concentrated on her birthday. It was as if the sun, the moon, and the stars stood still in preparation of *her* birthday. I could appreciate the excitement of anticipation because in Germany birthdays are big affairs, and I grew up as the youngest of four daughters in a family that believed in rituals and tradition.

As early as I can remember, my birthdays started with the family singing in front of my door. My father, barely dressed, would corral the family and hold forth in the bass, while my mother and sisters fell into the harmonies of a familiar song. They always ended with "*Wir gratulieren zum Geburtstag* [happy birthday]!" And then I would get up and review presents set up on the dining room table. From there the day would continue without ceremony until the afternoon when my mother would present a cake. I don't remember inviting friends to the afternoon *Kaffee und Kuchen*. I spent my early childhood during World War II when resources were scarce and it was a big deal to get a cake. Presents on the table were practical things, such as stockings and underwear, perhaps knitted from wool remnants and always itchy to the skin. I never received toys or games. I played with my one and only doll all the time, and sometimes my mother used scraps to sew new clothes for her.

We celebrated Maria's second birthday in grand style. I invited fifteen close friends, who had weathered with me the four-year adoption odyssey. The big rum cake came from Avignon Frères, the classy French restaurant and caterer that tried to survive in our predominantly Hispanic Adams Morgan neighborhood. I remember carefully balancing the cake in its square box with my left hand on one stroller handle, while pushing Maria with my right hand on the other handle. The four-block trip seemed longer than ever. At three in the afternoon, I changed Maria from overalls into a little dress of blue and white stripes and poured her sturdy legs into white pantyhose. She was surprisingly cooperative. Perhaps she sensed the significance of this momentous event: her first birthday in the United States, with her new mom and a family of friends. We were about to create a ritual that would last a lifetime.

Maria was excited as our friends arrived. She loved a full house. She ripped off the wrapping paper, flung alphabet magnets into the air, took puzzles apart, and swiftly assembled her first Lego blocks. She was passed from lap to lap, enjoyed tosses through the air, and amazed everyone with her huge capacity for birthday cake. We sat on the white *flokati* rug with my guitar making the rounds, introducing Maria to "Old McDonald" (had a farm) and "There Was an Old Woman" (who swallowed a fly)—the repertoire that would dominate our music making for the next several years.

She loved the fiesta! She charged after bouncing balloons with a flushed face until she was dripping wet from all the kicking, tossing, and turning, and only took time out for diaper changes. "What a kid," marveled our friends. Their wonder felt like a blessing that carried us beyond the day.

I remember Maria's birthdays as precious and exhausting. For her third birthday, she was allowed to invite three friends; for her fourth, four. And so it went up to age ten, when I suggested we had better start spiraling down. During the weeks leading up to January 24, her exuberance often turned into misbehavior, and I'd threaten to call the celebration off, unless … We battled over the shape and size of the affairs, revised scenarios, and compromised on lights-out during sleepovers. As she grew older, birthdays were often clouded by Maria's mood swings. While everyone was completely engaged in games and play, Maria would retreat into a corner. On her sixth birthday, for example, her best friend Heather organized an impromptu dramatic presentation. She gave the other girls their lines of the script, created a few props, and commenced the performance on the oak staircase of our big old house on Alaska Avenue, where we had moved when Maria was five.

As Heather announced the first act, I pulled my chair into the front row, asking Maria to join me in the audience. Instead, she curled up on the sofa, crying, "They are all different from me. I don't belong." The sense of abandonment and loss seemed to overwhelm her, especially on birthdays.

Years later, one of Maria's very talented and devoted counselors explained to me that birthdays were times of special turmoil for adopted children. "Thinking of their birth, they remember that they were let go," the counselor said. She knew. She had been adopted.

Another birthday

When people asked me how old Maria was when I adopted her, I usually said "two, *mas o menos* [more or less]." But she was possibly older, I discovered years later when I sorted a box of adoption documents I'd kept in the attic. The papers were in Spanish and bundled together. I had never taken time to study them line by line. One of them, I now discovered, listed Maria's age as three and a half at the time of adoption, instead of twenty months, as noted on her birth certificate. A big discrepancy! In shock, I sat on the attic steps, calculating that she'd be eight right now, instead of six and a half. At the time, she was completely ensconced in her group of first-graders. What should I do? Get a bone test to determine her true age? Make her skip two years of learning? Should I share my discovery with her? After a few sleepless nights, I decided to let her be six, according to the date in the passport. But I remember a poignant conversation from that time.

We were walking in the morning to our friend Rebecca's house where a maid supervised a number of neighborhood children for an hour before school started. It was October and the days were still warm enough for Maria's beige Bermudas and brown short-sleeve top. Her thick brown hair was gathered in a bouncing ponytail. She looked great, I thought, as we walked hand-in-hand down the tree-lined street.

"You know, sometimes I think I'm older," Maria said, and my heart skipped a beat.

"How old do you think you might be?" I asked with trembling voice.

"Maybe seven or eight."

"That's interesting," I said meekly, tempted to tell her about my attic discovery.

"Do you like being six?"

"It's okay," she said, and then changed the subject.

When she started menstruating at nine and a half we were both upset. She was attending summer camp at the Cathedral School when she came home one day with blood stains on her shorts. "You've got your period," I exclaimed in shock. "No, no," she cried, "I think I hurt myself." It took us a while to deal with the event. As I picked out the appropriate paraphernalia at the drugstore, I wondered again how old she really was. She was the first in her age group to enter this initiation into womanhood, and she hid the fact for years as best she could.

When she turned eighteen, I presented Maria with a box of adoption papers. As far as I know, she never scrutinized the documents that listed different birth dates.

In the end, it didn't matter.

January 24, 1979, is the birth date engraved in granite on her tomb stone.

4.

FATHERS AND FAMILY

When I decided to adopt, it never occurred to me that single parenting was deficient. Fathers were exciting, granted. But mothers made the world go round. I had done my research during childhood.

My father was often distant and distracted, and, when he stood in the pulpit, I sometimes confused him with God. He lived in a study lined with books and sat at a desk where he wrote and pondered. Between paragraphs, he paced back and forth, mumbling to himself. We had to knock and wait for his "*herein*" before we could enter to deliver a hasty message, such as "lunch is ready" or "you have a visitor."

I amazed my sisters by visiting Papa often. I remember reaching on tiptoes for the golden curved handle of his study door. I'd bring my little stool and explain, "I just want to stay with you for a while." He barely took note and continued writing, reading, and pacing while I studied the book I'd brought. We'd settle into companionable silence, but once in a while he'd stop and tell me to stand up "straight like a candle" so he could lift me by my ankles to the ceiling while I shuddered with excitement. Or he would place me on the top shelf to take in the scary view from above. Just when I thought he'd left me for good, he'd stop by my dangling feet and tell me to jump. That took courage and faith, but Papa always caught me in his arms.

There was a thrill to my father's games. Like when he played with my sister Claudia and me after lunch. He'd pull a chair to the wall and turn into a loudly snoring lion while we sneaked past him, terrified of being caught. When he did catch us, the lion would devour us with cuddles and kisses that were especially ticklish on the neck. We survived with giggles of exhaustion,

27

and then Papa would retreat again into the splendid isolation of his study or disappear altogether on frequent trips.

He was superintendent of a large district during the war and looked after churches whose pastors had been drafted into the army. During Papa's absences, our household relaxed into creative chaos. My mother—we called her Mutti, the equivalent of "Mom" in English—stayed in her blue housecoat all morning, cooked infrequently, rearranged furniture, and sewed us outfits from Papa's worn-down clerical frocks. She borrowed the scissors from his desk, as we all helped ourselves to his neatly assembled pencils, markers, erasers, and ruler. Hours before Papa's return, my mother participated in the mad scramble as we tried to locate his tools and restore them to their rightful place.

We often failed. Meals with the six of us assembled around the oval table would often start with Papa asking, "Who took my scissors?" Nobody had. Or he would hold up a towel, all wet with outlines of dirty little hands, "Who used my towel this morning?" Nobody had, of course, though we all preferred Papa's towel, clean and dry, in contrast to our shared, soggy linen cloths.

He set the tone and rituals of our household. At our *Mittagessen*, the main noon meal, we were to eat "as if the emperor were our guest." For Papa, born in Vienna, the emperor was a reference point. As a fourteen-year-old, while strolling through the parks of Schönbrunn, Papa had once greeted Kaiser Franz Josef at close range. They had made eye contact and the Kaiser had acknowledged the young student with a nod. So, because of the emperor, we sat with straight backs, ate without slurping and smacking, and learned to handle knife and fork with wrists hovering over the table's edge. Woe if you were caught slouching and sprawling! Claudia might sneak up on you, grab your elbow, and bang it on the table—ouch! If we grumbled over the food, Papa declared categorically, "What Mutti cooks tastes good!" And he was usually right.

During lunch, my father also liked to question my sisters—six, nine, and eleven years older than I—on their school performance. "What did you learn today, Claudia?" he'd inquire. But Claudia, a real tomboy, rarely remembered. He would jolt Heidi, a notorious daydreamer, into the here and now by shouting, "*Ziegenpeter!*" (German for mumps, which Heidi had endured bravely.) She sat next to Papa and had little to fear. She always studied her Latin, had an A in math, and, at the age of fourteen, became our church organist.

Bubbly Beate, the oldest, made Papa laugh with her *chutzpah*, like how she wiggled herself out of conscription into the Hitler Youth brigade. She was beautiful and very popular and secretly flirted with boys, despite the threat of incurring Papa's wrath. One time, when we were attending Engelbert Humperdinck's *Hansel and Gretel*, a boy approached my oldest sister with a casual "Hello, Beate," and Papa hit the young man for his brazen familiarity right there in the foyer of the theater. Beate was mortified. My mother, bless her, urged Papa to apologize. If he had had his way, Papa would have locked us all into medieval chastity belts by the time we started menstruating.

Our parents loved music, and songs usually started or concluded meals. Each of us got her turn asking for a favorite song, one of the few democratic moments in our family life. Supper always concluded with *"Breit aus die Flügel beide."* When I was a baby, my mother told me, I'd start sucking my thumb while rocking with the rhythm of the evensong.

My sisters keep telling me that I lived a charmed life. I can't see it that way. True enough, I escaped Papa's mealtime scrutiny because the last time we all sat around the table in Schneidemuehl, I had just started second grade and was still brilliant. But I was sick and tired of hand-me-downs and having to always share treats and goodies with three sisters.

"There are too many of us," I once complained.

"Well," said my mother, "then *you* should have stayed away."

"Not *I*," I countered, "but one of the others."

"Then who should have stayed away?" she asked.

I was hard pressed. Beate, often bossy, filled the house with lots of excitement. Heidi told me stories and let me sleep with her. Claudia, jealous at my birth, had become my closest buddy and cheerleader. And so I never answered my mother.

Mutti and I shared compatible mornings while my sisters were at school. She would spare small quantities of salt and sugar and berries of the season, so I could concoct dishes on a kitchen chair that served as "stove." We went shopping at the family grocery up the hill where I got treats of pickles or sauerkraut from the barrel. Mutti advised me on mothering my doll and taught me to sew with leftover snippets of cloth. Playing with my friends, I soon knew my housewife script by heart.

I had two boyfriends. Helmut lived with his grandparents in an elegant villa around the corner. There was something hushed-up about him, like why didn't he live with his parents? He was my age, very pampered, had great toys, and little imagination. I remember turning up at his house when I was about five. His grandfather consulted me whether Helmut should wear his rubber boots because it was drizzling. This boy had leather boots *and* rubber boots and all sorts of outerwear choices, while I had my one hand-me-down coat and boots that were pretty much worn through. I advised galoshes, as I recall. And then we would set out taking turns on Helmut's new yellow tricycle, or run to the nearby park, as Horstl, my other boyfriend, tried to catch up with us, yelling, "But Frau Kreutzer said *I* should play with you."

Horstl was a few months younger than I and had a little sister whom I adored. He was the son of the church custodian who was fighting for the fatherland on the Russian front. In his absence, my mother scrubbed the church. Horstl was a big bore and a coward to boot, as I discovered. Once, when he was in our kitchen, a bee flew through the unscreened window. "I have to go home now," he announced with fright written all over him. I saw right through him and my contempt sent him packing.

Horstl was correct, however, when he yelled that Frau Kreutzer wanted *him* to play with me. My mother considered him the safer of my choices, and, besides, his family belonged to our dwindling congregation and lived upstairs. Our friendship was meant to be an important symbol in these times of warring hostility. So, after I had run off with Helmut once too often, my mother locked Horstl and me into the garden with the stern advice to have a good time. I hated her. To complete my humiliation, Helmut paraded his beautiful tricycle at the fence with an air of pity for my confinement.

Gathering the remnants of my pride, I decided we should play house. With a stick, I drew the outline of our parish into the dirt. Here was the kitchen, there the bedrooms, the dining room, the blue salon, and the study. I commanded that Horstl should sit in the study while I went shopping, cooked, cleaned, hung the laundry, and aired the featherbeds.

Horstl complained that he was bored. "Think," I told him. "You sit at your desk and think! Or you can pace back and forth between the desk and the bookcases. And I'll call you when *Mittagessen* is ready." He didn't care for my stage directions, poor fellow, but I was happy and wonderfully busy. By the time my mother stuck her head through the kitchen window and threw us jam sandwiches for mid-morning snacks, I had almost forgotten that I hated her.

The patterns of our family life remained ingrained. What I learned in childhood I carried into adulthood: dads were thrilling at best and demanding at worst, and rather peripheral in between, while mothers quilted and mended the fabric of our everyday life. When feminism hit in the sixties, it confirmed my notion of equality. I felt perfectly comfortable with the idea of starting a family on my own. Of course I could raise a child! And wouldn't she be lucky having me for a mother!

Enter Maria.

She confounded me from day one with her distinct preference for men and her yearning for a father. She barely acknowledged my enthusiastic women friends who showered her with gifts and affection. Instead, she quivered with excitement when the plumber turned up to repair the radiator, and she would have walked off with the mailman had I not held her back.

When I placed her into the care of Marta, a Salvadoran woman, Maria hit it off especially well with the men in Marta's extended family. Marta lived with a husband and three school-age children in the basement apartment of a brownstone in our Hispanic neighborhood. She had a thriving business taking care of four toddlers still in diapers. Like me, the other mothers were desperate for a safe place for their children so they could pursue demanding careers. Marta was a kind and competent mom who didn't speak much English and was delighted that my little *Colombiana* understood *Español*. In fact, Maria soon became queen bee and was fussed over by Marta's whole clan. One friendly uncle enjoyed carrying Maria around, and I have lots of photos of the two of them clowning with sombreros and all sorts of hats. Maria was radiant.

When she turned three, I declared her toilet-trained (she wasn't and had lots of "accidents") and enrolled her in a preschool, the Barbara Chambers Children's Center, within walking distance of our co-op. The center was a relic from the sixties, founded on the idealism of racial and economic diversity. Middle-class parents paid a hefty fee so poorer children could attend with the help of scholarships. The result was rainbow-colored classrooms, staffed with English- and Spanish-speaking teachers.

Maria thrived at Barbara Chambers and especially loved painting boldly at the easel. In a significant drawing about her family, she grouped herself, her mom, and Joanie, her teacher, into the outline of a circle. The other children drew a dad into their family portraits, even if he was mostly absent. Only three of the ten children in the class came from two-parent households. Most lived with their mothers and saw their dads sometimes on weekends.

Their daddy-talk rubbed off on Maria. She was soon telling me, "I need to talk to my daddy," and I would hand her the telephone and she would tell him to be sure to pick her up after school on Friday. Talking to her daddy became an obsession. Whenever we passed a payphone, Maria would say that she needed to talk to her daddy now and we would pause so she could talk into the dead line. I went along with the game and didn't see a need to interrupt. Until one Sunday, when she declared with urgency that she had to leave now to meet her daddy.

It was a chilly day, and I helped her into her coat and hat. Surely she'd just leave the house and return promptly, I figured, and opened the heavy front door. Off she went, down the street. When she didn't stop I grabbed my coat and ran after her. "Is this your little girl?" inquired a passing woman with reproach in her voice. We didn't live in a neighborhood where three-year-olds could safely roam the streets. Maria was standing at the curb of an intersection when I caught up with her. She knew better than to cross by herself. As I called her, she turned with despair written across her sweet face, "I looked for him all over but I can't find him." It almost broke my heart. "I am so sorry," I said, kneeling down. And then wrapped her into my arms and carried her home.

That's when we had a serious talk.

"You know," I said, "the reason you don't have a daddy is because I am not married. If I would be married, you would have a dad."

"Then why don't you be married?" she inquired.

"Well, I don't really know a good man," I said defensively.

"Ha, ha," she laughed and then enumerated all the good men we knew, either married or gay or too young or a relative, like my good-looking nephew Mark who had charmed Maria during previous visits. I kept mumbling my excuses, but also encouraged her to help me find a suitable match. And that marked the end of Maria's daddy-fixation. When Father's Day approached, I told Joanie that Maria shouldn't be asked to make a Father's Day card.

"But every child has a father," Joanie objected. "Even if he is in California or Mexico."

"But Maria has no father, not even a distant one," I explained.

Joanie promised to think about that. On the Saturday before Father's Day Maria came home with a present for Sev, a fatherly friend. She had made him a clay dog. The next time we visited Sev and Mary, my good friends in Boston, Maria presented her gift. Sev was deeply touched and always ready to return Maria's affection.

Ten years later, when she was thirteen, Maria gave me a Father's Day card. It had a photo of a kitten nestling in a big hand and the printed message, "I know I'm in good hands with you, Daddy!" Maria had added: "Dear V, I know this is weird, but you are supposed to be my mother and my father. Happy Father's Day. You need some work on the father part, but I guess you're doing your best."

She was right; I was doing my best. But she missed the father part in me. "She wants you to drink more beer, kick back in a La-Z-Boy, and scream at the TV during ballgames," explained my friends with a laugh. Beer and sports were clearly not my style.

Instead of taking her to ballgames, I introduced Maria to Shakespeare. When she was eight I took her, all dressed up, to see *A Winter's Tale* at the Old Vic Theatre in Washington. I had fond memories of seeing the play at an outdoor theatre in Wannsee, Berlin, right after the war. The play tells the story about an insanely jealous king who suspects his loving wife of betrayal and orders his servant to kill her. The man can't do it and kills a deer instead, presenting the king with the deer's heart as proof of the killing. Meanwhile, he hides the queen in a safe place. Twenty years pass and the king feels remorse over his evil deed. He has a statue cast in the queen's memory and, at its unveiling, expresses sorrow—when suddenly the statue stirs to reveal the living queen. They live happily ever after. The end. Since my mother had raised me on fairy tales, this story fired my imagination as a young girl. But the magic was lost on Maria.

She squirmed in her wooden seat and begged to go home. I could barely placate her with an enormous cookie during intermission. On the way home, she announced that she'd had it with Shakespeare. "Stupid play," she said. "And the king was wrong. That stupid queen shouldn't have forgiven him!" She had a point.

Maria scored even more points on the soccer field. She was six when she started playing in a group of first graders at Shepherd Park Elementary School, our neighborhood's public school. Maria's team had been organized by Janice Grand, the mother of Barbara, who had also been adopted in Colombia. In addition to Barbara, Janice and her husband had also adopted a younger Colombian boy. They lived a few blocks from Alaska Avenue, and soon became part of our support system. On Saturdays, Janice gathered the first graders on the school's athletic field and tried to teach them soccer rules, yelling, "No, you can't use your hands, and don't hog the ball, and don't push each other." The girls mostly ignored her, followed their instincts, and moved like undulating amoebas across the field.

By second grade, the group joined a Maryland network of soccer teams that met on Saturday mornings for weekly competitions. Thousands of girls played on dozens of fields throughout mostly white suburbia. Our integrated team of black, Hispanic, and white girls frequently met with racial slurs and hostility from players on the other teams. Janice was vigilant and insisted on apologies from red-faced coaches.

Little by little, the girls learned about team spirit, cooperation, and trust. From the sidelines, I admired and envied their experience. Women of my generation hadn't had the opportunity to play team sports. At work, I noticed how easily men, used to team play, threw the "ball" toward each other while women had no clue how to participate in these competitive office games.

My daughter was a natural on the soccer field and became one of the team's best players. When she was eight, she was encouraged to try out for a DC team that was preparing for friendly competitions in our sister city, Beijing, China. However, when we turned up for tryouts, we were told this was for boys only. "That's unfair," cried Maria, collapsing into tears. I agreed and sent a note of protest to the city council. At eight, I argued, there is no difference between the athletic ability of boys and girls. This was a case of sex discrimination, I noted. The city council agreed and withdrew support from the team. But the team went to Beijing anyway with corporate blessings and private funding. *The Washington Post*'s Metro section took note of the soccer outing and also mentioned Maria Kreutzer's tearful cry of foul. She grinned when we read the story, but, later, when we were riding in the car she wondered, "Does everyone know me now?" And when I teasingly said, "Yes, they sure do," she cried, "Oh no," and slipped from her seat to the floor, lest any passing car notice her.

When the World Cup came to the DC area in 1994, I got hot tickets through my State Department connections and sent Maria with our friend Sam to the Mexican game. I had known Sam's wife, Nancy, since graduate school days in Massachusetts, and "Samanancy," as Maria came to call them in one breath, had remained close friends. Sam was an enthusiastic sports spectator who normally thought and taught political science, but, when he went off with Maria, Sam liked to regress into stats talk and sports lingo.

The Colombians had sent an excellent team with hopes of winning the Cup. With Sam and Nancy, we watched a decisive game against the United States on a big screen at a neighborhood sports bar. The place was packed with Latinos who screamed their *Olé*s with beer-soaked fervor. The Colombian goalie, with his wild hair and good looks, had become a superhero and my daughter's heartthrob. We were all rooting for the Colombian team, partly for Maria's sake. For once, her birth country was excelling in an international forum, and she felt so proud. And then disaster struck: Andrés Escobar, a defender, scored an own goal (a goal that counted against his own team), and the United States went on to win, 2–1. The Colombian team was subsequently eliminated. *Qué lástima!* [What a shame!]

Little did we know then how the game would really end. When the team returned to Bogota, Andrés Escobar was gunned down and killed outside a bar in a Medellin suburb. There were rumors that the team had been financed by drug lords who hadn't been able to stomach their gambling losses. It was a sobering reminder that Colombia was the most violent country in our hemisphere.

Maria's enthusiasm for soccer continued, even after two knee surgeries. When she attended the American School in Vienna, Austria, her team once took the Orient Express to Budapest to compete. Soccer took Maria many places, including the front page of the *Philadelphia Inquirer*'s sports section, which featured Maria Kreutzer with bandaged knee fighting for her team at Solebury, the boarding school in Pennsylvania from which she eventually graduated. She remained a jock at heart. To catch the ball, she'd throw herself into mud and puddles with abandon, returning home encrusted like a mummy. She'd luxuriate under a hot shower, emerging with her long hair dripping wet. She'd hop onto the kitchen counter to tell me stories from the field while I negotiated pots and pans around her in preparation for a dinner party.

I confess that I was often missing from the sidelines. Whenever Janice offered to chauffeur kids from the neighborhood, I gratefully accepted so that I could have an extra six hours in my Saturday. My government job took me away from the house for eleven hours daily, and my weekends were filled with laundry, cleaning, mowing the lawn, and grocery shopping. Our 1927, four-bedroom house with a rental unit in the basement demanded lots of my attention. I spent many Saturdays traipsing to Hechinger's, DC's home-care hub, trying to find the right brackets for the broken rail or washers for the dripping faucets.

So I missed a lot of games and moments of Maria's glory on the field. When she turned into a hostile teenager, she added my no-shows to her long list of grievances. The father part in me was sorely lacking. I secretly envied my divorced friends whose ex's would loyally take care of children on alternate weekends. Heather, Maria's best friend, for example, spent every other weekend, rain or shine, with Dad. Though I never developed an appetite for marriage, despite passionate affairs, I sometimes fantasized about putting an ad into the personals. "Wanted: Divorced husband who's crazy about the child, yells his heart out at her ball games, and takes enthusiastic care of her every other weekend." Wimp that I am, I never placed the ad.

Over the years, Maria talked less frequently about wanting a dad. I remember a long evening talk when she was twelve and we were living in Vienna. She had come into my room and plunked herself on my bed where I was reading a book about the enlightened Austrian Emperor Josef I.

"I wish I had a dad," she said, as I placed the marker and closed my book.

"What should he be like?" I asked.

She had a hard time listing his qualities, but he should definitely be interested in sports.

We made a list of all the men we knew, wondering who would be a good dad. Most of them flunked for one reason or another—except John Grand, Barbara's dad. Maria had observed him up close that summer when she had stayed with the Grands for a week during her month of home leave in the United States. Yes, John was a great dad, I agreed. But he was Barbara's. It was a moment of profound sadness for Maria. She had to come to terms with the realization that in this life we cannot always have what we think we need. We either make do with what there is or despair over what's missing.

In the end, Maria's need for a dad went underground. From the diary she left behind, I learned that she had made up a whole new family, more real than her single mom in Seattle. She even introduced new friends to the characters of her fantasy. Her parents hadn't gotten along and were divorced, she told her boyfriend's parents. Her father still lived in Colombia. In one entry of her diary, Maria wrote that she was gathering courage to call her father. Alas, she hadn't been able to connect with him, she wrote sadly.

I've been reeling from these revelations ever since I read Maria's diary on the day of her funeral. I speculate that she had and knew a family at birth. During early adolescence, her need to resurrect parents and siblings turned desperate. She longed to fix her fate.

Flower girl at a cousin's wedding in Germany

5.

"WHERE DO I BELONG?"

Sometimes I wonder what my life would have been like if I had been swept off my German feet at three and taken to … let's say, China. Different faces, different cuisine, different language. Would I have adjusted and eventually blended in, or would I have kept looking for my German tribe and roots?

As it turned out, I *am* a transplant. I came to the United States at the age of twenty-two on a Greek boat that took ten days to cross the Atlantic. When we passed the fogged-in Statue of Liberty on a September morning in 1959, I was ready to embark on my American adventure with two suitcases and bags of curiosity.

I was headed for graduate study at Duke University in Durham, North Carolina. My father had helped me get there. After his retirement from the ministry, he had traveled for several months throughout the United States, invited by old family friends and former GIs who had spent many hours at our home in Berlin right after the war.

Karl Kreutzer preached and lectured his way from coast to coast in sturdy boots and with a rucksack, traveling by Greyhound and Trailways, often overnight to save money on hotels. He knew enough English to hold forth, because he had once served a German congregation in London right after graduating from seminary in Frankfurt. In his theology, my father was a follower of Karl Barth, one of the great Christian thinkers of the twentieth century. Barth's monumental, 9,000-page *Church Dogmatics* lined Papa's bookshelves, and Barth's ideas often sparked hair-splitting dinner talk. Do angels exist? Certainly! Barth has a thick section on angelology. Can humans know God? Yes, says Barth, but only through revelation. Barthian thinking and experiences during two world wars fueled Papa's sermons and lectures during his American sojourn.

After a guest lecture at Duke's Divinity School, my father inquired whether they might have a scholarship for his youngest daughter, a schoolteacher in the Black Forest. They did, and, six months later, I arrived on the Duke campus at the graduate women's dorm, Epworth Inn, a colonial building that looked like a movie set from *Gone with the Wind.*

My American education commenced as much from books and lectures as from the budding civil rights movement. I was appalled by the segregation and racism that surrounded me. *Is this the America that brought us democracy?* I wondered. Some of my fellow students were among the first to get arrested at lunch counters in Greensboro. At one point, seven hundred Duke students were in jail for trying to integrate Howard Johnson's on the highway between Durham and Chapel Hill. I participated in kneel-ins at segregated churches, shuttled picketers and demonstrators in my blue VW bug, and sang "We Shall Overcome" at rallies in black churches.

I was careful, however, not to get arrested—and possibly deported— because I was falling in love with America and all the good people who were putting their lives on the line for the noble cause of integration. I wanted to become part of this American diversity, because there had been none where I had grown up. It was my privilege to help integrate Duke when the faculty voted to admit the first black students to the all-white school.

By then I was a full-time instructor in the German department, after receiving a master's in comparative literature with a minor in religion. I had launched my U.S. career at the right time, it turned out. A new educational policy mandated the study of foreign languages in the aftermath of Sputnik, the Soviet Union's first satellite. Sputnik spurred the United States to invest great resources into the space program with the goal of landing a person on the moon. I'm not sure how learning languages contributed to that goal, but colleges began to require undergraduates to take at least two years of a foreign language. Institutions of higher learning were desperate to fill teaching positions and I was hired, at the age of twenty-three, to instruct second-year Duke students in my mother tongue.

I admit that they didn't get their money's worth. The students surprised me with all sorts of rules that I hadn't ever contemplated, such as the effect of coordinating and subordinating conjunctions on a verb's position in a sub-clause. German was full of pitfalls, I noticed. I knew my mother tongue very well, of course, but had no clue how to teach it as a foreign language.

Ten years later, I did my penance at Houghton Mifflin in Boston when I edited *German Today,* a best-selling series of text books. I wrote, rewrote, and edited rules about word order and the subtle use of the subjunctive, always with a mental *mea culpa* to my first Duke students who had known better than I.

By then I was in my early thirties, living off Harvard Square in a lovely brownstone with two fireplaces, down the street from a family grocery where Julia Child, towering and regal, did the shopping for her TV gourmet show. Life was good, except for love affairs that left me wanting. It occurred to me that perhaps I wasn't the marrying type, but what about children? I have always loved children. As a ten-year-old in Berlin, I would knock on neighbors' doors and ask if I could take their little kids to the park, push them on the swing, and line them up for games. At twelve, I abandoned my doll in favor of playing with my first-born niece. Among the offspring in my family, I remained a favorite aunt. But I wanted a child of my own. There were so many unwanted and neglected children in this world, why couldn't I have one? And then one morning, a story on public radio moved me in the right direction. It told about the first single woman in Massachusetts who had succeeded in adopting a child. I could do that, I realized, sitting on my unmade bed. By the time I'm thirty-five, I vowed, I'll adopt a child.

It so happened that I celebrated my thirty-fifth birthday in a tent on safari in Tanzania. My fellow celebrants were two handsome tennis players from California who were competing on the East African circuit while also taking time to see the sights. We had met in November on the Greek island of Crete. Matt, the taller of the two, and I had fallen for each other playing on the beach. "See you in Nairobi," we promised when we separated a few weeks later in Athens. I was headed for Lebanon, Syria, Egypt, and down the Nile to the Sudan, while the two guys went ahead to East Africa to buy a van and camping equipment for their long trek through eastern and southern Africa.

On my birthday, we had a romantic candle-lit dinner while camping on Tanzania's Serengeti Plains. Giraffes nimbly nibbled the leaves off a thorn tree next to our tent. Sudden roaring noises in the distance made the giraffes perk their ears and flee, half galloping, half flying. We had pitched our tent despite the warning signs and felt impervious to danger. It was my birthday, after all, and we lifted our glasses in praise of Africa's immense beauty and the goodness of its people.

"What do you plan to do with the rest of your life?" Matt inquired, mocking my old age, since he was a few years younger. I had no clue. Adopting a daughter had become a dream postponed, at least during this year of travels with a backpack, a sleeping bag, and my diaphragm. I still had to climb Mt. Kilimanjaro, visit a kibbutz in Israel, sail on the Mediterranean to Venice, and see the Matisse chapel in the South of France.

Back in Nairobi, I found a letter from my sister Heidi in the stack of mail at the American Express. Heidi wrote that her choral society in Pforzheim, Germany, had raised funds for a technical school on the shores of Kenya's Lake Turkana. Perhaps I could find out about that project and write a story, she said, gently suggesting that my single-minded pursuit of happiness could use direction.

Consulting my map, I discovered shallow, crocodile-infested Lake Turkana in the arid Rift Valley at Kenya's northern border. A bus from Nairobi took me to a little farming town at the end of the paved road. From there, English settlers advised, I could proceed only via bush plane or the occasional lorry that took cement to the lake and brought back dried fish. The settlers cautioned against taking the lorry. A white man who had recently boarded it had disappeared without a trace. But, since I didn't have the money for a plane, I decided to wait for the lorry. When it finally arrived, I was the only white passenger and the only woman among the tall Turkanas, who wore loincloths and carried sticks. They climbed to the top and arranged themselves on the cement bags, and when I started to climb after them, the friendly driver motioned for me to sit with him in the cab. At rest stops, the men politely averted their eyes and let me pee behind the ever-scarcer bushes. The trip took two days and a night through desert and dried riverbeds. When we arrived at the lake, coated with dust and rattled to the bones, I was greeted by a gregarious American couple, who had been sent by the American Friends Service Committee to help build the technical training center at the southern tip of the lake. Some of the international funding for the center had come from my sister's choir group.

The friendly Quakers offered me cold water from the only fridge for hundreds of miles and let me roll out my sleeping bag on their patio under a starry sky. For the next few days, I observed how cement turns into walls, I interviewed African workers and potential students, and I visited an elementary school under a thatched roof. Back in Nairobi, I wrote my story in two languages and got it published on two continents.

I soon discovered other stories. They went into a growing portfolio of publications and eventually paved the way for a job as writer and broadcaster with the Voice of America (VOA) in Washington DC. Working in the nation's capital had been my goal upon return after a year of explorations in the wider world.

VOA's background check took a year. Investigators wanted to know exactly when and where I had been in Salzburg, giving the impression that the Austrian border town was a scenic and sizzling hub of spying during the cold war. They requested names and addresses of relatives I had visited in communist Hungary and Yugoslavia. "Did you ever have intercourse behind the iron curtain?" they asked bluntly. "Let me think," I said. My anti-Vietnam war activities raised eyebrows, but, in the end, the snoops concluded that I wasn't un-American.

At "the Voice," I broadcast in German for RIAS (Radio In the American Sector), the first Berlin radio station established by the Americans after the war. In August of 1945, my family and I had settled as refugees in Berlin's rubble, and RIAS had been our primary source of political and cultural information. As a teenager I listened religiously to *Schlager der Woche*, the weekly hit parade. I couldn't have dreamed then that I would serve one day as a foreign correspondent for RIAS. Some of the Washington-produced reports and features were also beamed from other German-language stations, including Austrian radio. My Viennese cousin Elfi said she heard me regularly.

Like most broadcast networks in the seventies, VOA was a citadel of sex discrimination. While my male colleagues reported and commented on hard-hitting news, I got the so-called "softer" stories, such as Betty Ford's breast cancer. To avoid the daily humiliations, I branched out into thirty-minute documentaries in the vein of today's National Public Radio program *All Things Considered*. I wrote about women in politics, for example, and the needs and opportunities of a graying America. I wrote about the history and accomplishments of America's labor movement, the challenges of an education for all, and especially enjoyed cultural themes, such as the renaissance of ragtime music.

Later, I joined the magazine staff and the Latin American press service at VOA's parent organization, the United States Information Agency (USIA). My perspective as a foreign-born citizen, I've always felt, gave me a special vantage point from which to tell America's story, "warts and all." This was, after all, USIA's mission, as defined by Ed Murrow, USIA's director during the Kennedy administration. While I adopted America as my new home, my perspective and curiosity remained global.

When my search for a child led me abroad, I realized that an international adoption suited my politics. The Kreutzer clan could use an infusion of different DNA, I reasoned. There had been something predictable about our family's offspring: They usually sprouted blond curls, put their noses into books as soon as they could read, loved music, and avoided competitive sports. Maria's looks and talents added pepper to the family's salty sameness.

"Look at that beautiful hair," my mother marveled when I presented Maria that first summer after the adoption. "What beautiful hair," she kept saying, stroking Maria's thick, black tresses. My mother's gray hair was thinning, and she spent most of her time sitting in her wing chair by the balcony. Despite the onset of dementia, her sense of beauty was still intact.

But her engagement in family life was much diminished, and her days of stellar storytelling were long past. She had raised two generations in the oral traditions of "Once upon a time …," and I sadly realized that Maria had missed Grandma in her prime.

We visited my father at the cemetery, and Maria skipped around the ivy on his grave.

"This is your granddaughter, Papa," I told him. "You always wanted a son and heir. And now this little waif from Bogota will carry your name into the next generation." I thought of him chuckling over this curious twist of fortune.

During Maria's first summer in Germany, my family rolled out the red carpet. Beate borrowed a stroller and set up a wading pool in her garden in Kaiserslautern. Heidi, musical and gifted with children, retrieved her basket of Orff instruments and marveled at Maria's attention span and rhythm. (Twentieth-century German composer Carl Orff developed a system of music education for children.) My niece Gabriele, who had two preschool children, provided playmates and a respite when I hiked with my sisters in the Black Forest. Maria, still very clingy, was happy to stay with her cousins and casually waved good-bye. Nico, half a year younger, liked to pursue her with kisses. A photo shows him in *Lederhosen* bending with a smooch over a reluctant Maria.

When we returned to DC and had finished unpacking, Maria said, "Let's go Ate [Beate]," not realizing that a nine-hour flight separated us from our relatives. But we stayed connected through gifts and greetings, and diligently saved vacation time and money for our next trip. We managed to travel to Germany every other year, several times also in the context of my business trips. While I consulted and worked in Africa, Maria stayed with relatives and attended summer camps in the Black Forest. She quickly became fluent in German juvenile lingo, including the expletives, and was a hit at family gatherings, when she flaunted her new expertise.

During alternate summers, we flew to Vancouver Island to visit my sister Claudia and her family. Claudia, an outdoor enthusiast and accomplished potter, seemed to have found her match. She would work with Maria in the studio by the water and then they'd jump into the icy bay in the noonday heat. Maria would be the first to float with swimming rings around her arms. "It's—just—right," she would assure us between gasps. "Your heart may stop for a few seconds," my sister explained before she dove in, "but if it's any good, it will start again." Reluctantly, I'd eventually follow. It was Claudia who taught Maria how to swim and dive.

With cousins in Germany

Despite the distance, my family was always close and important to me, and my loyalties rubbed off on Maria. She soon could name all members of the family and count them off on her fingers. "I have ten cousins," she informed one of them, little Janis, at one of our family reunions. He looked surprised. Family was a given to him and it hadn't occurred to him to count its members. But Maria obsessed about family and her adoption. I kept notes on three episodes from her seventh year, illustrating her lifelong struggle and ambivalence:

Six-forty a.m. in the bathroom. Maria is brushing her thick hair.

"I have trouble knowing about who is in my family. Children and uncles and everybody."

"But you know them all so well. You know you have ten cousins, and aunts and uncles."

"But I mean my real family."

"Oh, you mean your first family in Bogota."

With a bright smile, "Yeah, you know what I mean."

"Yeah. Now I know what you mean."

"I don't know who they are."

"Well, what do you think? What kind of family did you have?"

"A bad family."

"What do you mean?"

"Well, I was sick and they didn't take care of me. And they left me in the bathroom."

"Yes, but it wasn't their fault that they were poor."

"It wasn't *my* fault either."

"No, it wasn't. But you really would like to know about them."

"Yeah. That's my problem."

And then we discuss how she wants to have her hair braided. Eventually I give her a kiss, tell her that I love her, and send her off to school. She walks to the back gate, runs back to hand me *The Washington Post* she'd found there, and then we proceed with our day.

There were other times during that year when the adoption topic came up. At the YMCA summer camp, for example:

When I come to pick her up one evening, she wants me to meet a new friend. The little girl's parents are also just picking her up. I introduce myself and shake hands with the new friend. Maria pulls me down and whispers in my ear, "Tell her that I'm adopted; she doesn't believe me."

So I say, "Maria is adopted." The little girl stares. "Have you ever met anyone who has been adopted?" She shakes her head, apparently too stunned to talk. Her parents giggle nervously. "Well, now you know someone who has been adopted."

As we walk away, I ask Maria, "Do you like to tell people that you are adopted?"

"Of course," she says. "Adopted means that you are special."

Another time, CBS's Dan Rather announced that we would hear about adoption disclosure after the commercial:

"Let's listen," I say.

It's a story about the legal rights of adoptees to find their birth parents, despite sealed documents. Afterwards Maria says, "Well, that's all different from my story. I don't even know her. I hate her. She left me in the sink."

"In the sink?"

"Well, I don't know. I can't remember." She's impatient, very near tears, and quickly changes the subject.

During the twenty years of our life together, Maria was forever searching for her true family. There was the mystery of her twin. He turned up the first time she attended Deal Junior High School.

"There's a new boy in my grade," she reported. "Everybody says he looks like me. We may be twins." When I inquired further, it turned out that the boy was from El Salvador and was living with his biological parents. But, a few years later, Maria told an admissions counselor at Chelsea School that she had a twin brother, but he wasn't living with her. As a young adult Maria called him Emilliano Chapa and confided her sorrows and secrets into a diary dedicated to him.

"This book I write to my twin, my other half, my best friend, my brother," she wrote in the diary she left behind. "For twenty years you have been there for me ..."

To me, Emilliano remains a mystery.

But Rosa, her "sister," was real.

She was twelve—ten years older than Maria—when we met her, my daughter's first and favorite babysitter. She was born in El Salvador and lived in a low-rent high-rise in our Adams Morgan neighborhood. Her mother had come to the United States with a Foreign Service couple and had eventually brought her four children. Rosa's mother knew little English, even after a decade in DC, and worked as a domestic. At night she cleaned downtown offices and Rosa helped scrub bathrooms and vacuum plush carpets as part of the invisible crew that sanitizes corporate America. On weekends, Rosa sold her mom's delicious tamales on Columbia Road, the neighborhood's pulsing artery. While selling patties wrapped in cornhusks, she also learned to fend off leering advances from notorious drunks.

She was an exceptionally mature and responsible girl who laughed easily, even at Maria's temper tantrums. "What would you like to eat?" she'd say, opening the fridge to let Maria choose. Her high energy matched Maria's, and observing them playing, eating, and sleeping together made me wonder whether teenage motherhood was really such a bad idea. Our relationship started with a few hours here and there, and soon evolved into outings and compatible weekends. Our friends came to expect Rosa in our living room during holiday celebrations, and Maria began calling Rosa "my sister."

I trusted Rosa completely. When my nasty flu turned into pneumonia, it was seventeen-year-old Rosa who hailed a taxi and took me to Georgetown University Hospital. During my weeklong recovery there, Rosa took care of Maria at home. She cooked ("Terrible food, Mom," Maria later confided), checked homework, and dropped Maria at school before heading to her bilingual high school. By then she often stayed with us for longer, sometimes unscheduled, periods. There were late nights when Rosa called in desperation, or stood in front of our door because her older brother, in and out of jail, had been beating her and throwing her belongings out the window. Her mother was usually in an alcoholic stupor and of little help during these rampages. Rosa would stay with us for a few days and return home once tempers had cooled.

Her mother was, in turns, grateful and angry over our close relationship. One time she forbade Rosa to ever work for me again. That was after I got Rosa a summer job washing windows in our six-unit co-op. For over a month, Rosa maneuvered double-hung windows that hadn't moved much since the building went up in 1927. She crouched precariously on windowsills while salsa blasted from a boom box, and hired a friend to share both work and bounty. Once she got paid, she spent every penny in a flash. Her mother was furious—why hadn't she contributed to the household and saved a little? No more babysitting for Valerie! I went to visit them in their meticulously clean and neat apartment, and tried to negotiate between the warring parties. "Okay," said Rosa, "next time I won't spend it all." This was a difficult promise for a fifteen-year-old who lived below the poverty line.

Rosa was pretty and petite. She wore her second-hand clothes as if they were *haute couture*, and coifed her luscious black hair in braids and twists with style. "I'm going to be a hairdresser," she said. "No, you're not," I objected. "You're smart enough to go to college and pursue a bigger dream."

Sometimes Rosa was on the verge of quitting school, but, despite the turmoil at home, she graduated from the high school in our neighborhood. Maria and I sat in the audience when the group of immigrant children sang Michael Jackson's "We Are the World." Swaying in their black caps and gowns to the song's rhythm, they rendered but a timid version of its ebullient message:

> *We are the world*
> *We are the children*
> *We are the ones who make a brighter day*
> *So let's start giving*
> *There's a choice we're making*
> *We're saving our own lives*
> *It's true, we'll make a better day*
> *Just you and me.*

Maria and I applauded madly as tears streamed down my face. For some reason—was it work?—Rosa's mother didn't turn up for the occasion. With help from a committed school counselor, Rosa had won a scholarship to Trinity College, the excellent women's school next door to DC's Catholic University of America. Come September, she moved into a neo-Gothic dormitory on campus as one of a few minority students. On weekends, she often helped her mother, who was overwhelmed by yet another baby from yet another man. When she returned to school on the 7:00 a.m. bus on Mondays, Rosa was surrounded by Hispanics heading for janitorial jobs. "They're scrubbing the toilets and mopping my room," she observed. "It makes me feel weird. They are my people, but I feel like I've crossed a line."

She continued to spend time with us. Lying in the hammock in our garden, she'd dutifully underline passages in her psychology and sociology texts, trying hard to grasp abstract and unfamiliar concepts. Her heart wasn't in the liberal arts curriculum the good nuns had developed for her. She was more interested in design and drawing, and, at the end of her freshman year, she decided to transfer to the Maryland Institute of Art in Baltimore. The nuns were disappointed. They had hoped to wrest this girl from dysfunctional family life and the quagmire of poverty.

I supported Rosa's move and drove her to Baltimore to help her get settled. She had to proceed on student loans, because her mother refused to sign an application for financial aid. "My mom doesn't put her signature on anything," Rosa explained with a shrug.

She found work as a hostess in a popular restaurant, and, when she calculated her budget and found that she was still short by $50 a month, I promised to fill the gap. For the next three years, Rosa received my monthly check and a letter of encouragement.

"You know, you owe me," I once said half joking. "When Maria turns into an unruly teenager, I'll send her to you and you'll have to straighten her out."

"Sure," Rosa promised with a laugh.

We were both convinced that Maria's trip through adolescence would be rocky. But by then, Rosa would be settled in New York, making good money as an avant-garde designer. Neon signs were her passion, and we envisioned Rosa Ramón signatures in outrageous colors illuminating the Big Apple—yeah! But when Maria turned thirteen, Rosa disappeared from our lives without a telephone number or a forwarding address.

Years later, Maria told David's mother that she had a twin who had died, and an older sister who was an artist and lived in Baltimore. But her sister had disappeared into the black hole of drugs and crime, Maria told Natasha. And part of that story was true.

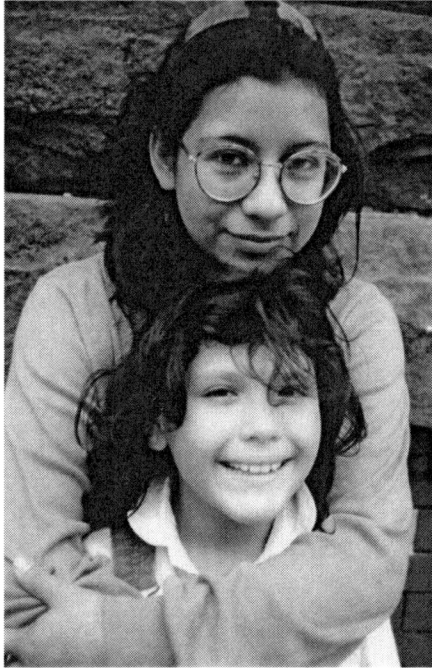

With an older "sister"

6.

HER SMARTS

I knew from day one that she was smart. The way she could concentrate on a game and respond to instructions told me that her faculties were intact. She didn't like to play alone and needed a partner, preferably an adult. The fear of abandonment was clearly in her bones. So we rolled the ball between us, made Lego towers, and drew messy pictures with finger paint. Hers always had more pizzazz than mine.

Maria also loved jigsaw puzzles with a passion. She received her first puzzle from visiting Canadian friends who worried that she might still be a bit too young for it. The puzzle depicted flowers with colorful petals against a black background. It was rubbery, and Maria took it easily apart and then squished the pieces back into their proper grooves without much ado. Soon the petals went in and out in record time, and the first puzzle was joined by a whole stack of new ones.

"When I grow up, I will have a puzzle factory," she announced at four, coming home from day care, where Joanie had apparently discussed career choices and professional options. She was going to make lots of jigsaw puzzles in a factory, Maria explained. What a far-fetched idea, I marveled. When tests eventually showed Maria's genius-level IQ in sequential thinking, it became clear why solving puzzles was her lifelong passion. She started simply enough, but soon increased to puzzles with a few hundred, a thousand, and even two thousand pieces. That's when she lost me at the table. I'd forever try to piece together Van Gogh's yellow bed in Arles while Maria quickly assembled the rest of his room. I was a real loser.

I also lost at Memory, a game of finding matching drawings on cards that lie face down. The challenge is to find a matching pair and remember from previous attempts where the missing shoe or chair might be. Maria always collected the pairs quickly, towering over my meager bounty. Even when we played Scrabble, she won. I'd painstakingly spell my words to start a grid and then Maria, who couldn't spell worth a damn, would add a few letters here and there—including hard-to-place z's and q's—and triple her score.

When a psychiatrist who evaluated ten-year-old Maria suggested that we play more board games together to mollify her oppositional streak, I confessed that I really didn't enjoy those games because she always won. "That's impossible," he said, reminding me that I was about to become editor of an international magazine. Well, the good doctor hadn't seen the test scores. My middling intelligence was no match for Maria's superb spatial reasoning skills.

Although I failed miserably at jigsaw puzzles, I was pretty good at puzzles of the mind and hoped to share my own passion for books. I remember the first time I invited her to have a look at one. She threw the book clear across the room, causing the pages to flip and twist. What fun, let's do that again! Never mind the ritual of turning pages and looking at the caterpillar that ate itself into a butterfly. As we tossed books, I realized that she had probably never seen one before. The orphanage had been bare bones, and wherever she had spent her first years—some hut with corrugated metal for a roof, if that much—didn't contain a library, for sure.

In time, we turned the pages of all the children's classics, including Margaret Wise Brown's *Goodnight Moon*. Its message became a nighttime ritual. With Maria on piggyback, we walked through our apartment saying goodnight to the piano, the plants, and the teddy bears. But stories, whether read or told, were clearly not of interest.

I, on the other hand, had grown up on a steady diet of stories. When playing with Helmut and Horstl, I often suggested that we ask my mother to tell us a story for a change of pace. She'd be in the kitchen cooking or in the little blue room sewing, and she never turned us down.

"Would you like a story from the Bible or a fairy tale?" she'd ask and then commence with Moses crossing the Red Sea or a Hans Christian Anderson fairy tale. "The Little Match Girl" was my favorite because the bareheaded and barefoot girl, red and blue from cold, made me feel so very snug in the comforts of my home and hearth.

Once in a while, I'd have to interrupt my mother.

"No, first she said …," I'd correct her.

"Yes, you are right," she'd agree, "First she said …"

Eventually, she'd get us to the match girl's heavenly ending, all the while not missing a stitch on her treadle machine.

My mother told stories in four languages. She was born in a German enclave in Yugoslavia and spoke German at home and at church. At school she first learned Hungarian, then Serbo-Croatian, then quickly became fluent in English while attending an American college. When my sister Claudia's children were born in England, our mother told the Brothers Grimm fairy tales in English, often inserting key phrases in German.

"What did the wolf say to the little goats?" we'd prompt my four-year-old nephew Mark when he came to visit us in Germany.

"*Macht mir auf, ihr lieben Kinderchen, eure liebe Mutti ist da und hat euch was Schönes mitgebracht* [Open the door, my darlings, your dear mother is here and brought you something wonderful]," Mark would say to a chorus of appreciative laughter. He was a real hit with that phrase on the playground and learned German within a week.

When I tried to continue the oral tradition with my daughter, my attempts fell on deaf ears. During our first visit to the Barbara Chambers Children's Center, Joanie had all the children nicely assembled on a rug as she held up a book and turned its colorful pages. Maria didn't care to join the group. Instead, she was exploring every niche and corner of the magic room. *How could she miss out on a story?* I worried. But Joanie assured me that Maria's behavior was quite appropriate during a first visit. Undoubtedly, she'd soon sit there mesmerized with the rest of them. Little did we know that Maria's dislike for story time was linked to difficulties with verbal decoding.

She learned to speak English at three, pronouncing her words very clearly. "She talks just like you," observed a friend, commenting on my distinctive German-accented English. Maria delighted me with her very literal understanding of language.

There were the tulips, for example. A springtime bunch on the coffee table, welcoming our weekend. Maria gazed at them in wonder. "They are tulips," I explained. She promptly started pointing, "Tulips, three lips, five lips, seven lips ..." "No, just tulips." She looked at me blankly.

Another time I cut an orange and a pit fell out.

"That's a vitamin seed," she explained.

"A what?"

"A vitamin seed. Joanie says that oranges have vitamin seeds."

"Oh, you mean vitamin C. Yes, oranges have vitamin C like in Consuelo. But that's a pit."

"Well, where is the C?"

"You can't see it."

"Because the eyes are bigger?"

"Yes," I said with exasperation, short of a proper answer.

"Is today tomorrow?" was another of Maria's unanswerable questions, first thing in the morning. "Yes, today is what we said yesterday would be tomorrow," I'd say. "Tell me again," she'd counter. And if an explanation was really difficult, she'd say, "Tell me one more time."

She would listen carefully to words and their inflections. When I brought her a pink T-shirt from a Miami business trip, she declared proudly, "My mommy brought me this from her ami."

The summer before kindergarten she attended summer camp at the Cathedral School, a haven for Washington's brightest and richest. Paulette, the activist director of Barbara Chambers Children's Center, had secured a few slots for her minority children, and shuttled the group every day for enrichment to the Cathedral's green pastures.

"We have a silence teacher," Maria reported.

"What does she teach?" I asked, wondering if Maria was learning to meditate.

"She shows us how wood swims on the water and stones go under."

"Oh, a science teacher!"

"Yes, a silence teacher."

That fall we flew to Boston to visit friends and drove to Rockport, a lovely seaside town. As we watched the spectacle of thrashing waves, Maria fell silent. "What makes that?" she asked. I mumbled something about the wind and the magnetic pull of the sun and the moon. She kept staring, and, after a long silence, she said, "No, I know what makes the waves."

"You do?"

"Yes, the fish push the water to the beach and then they turn around and push it right back." That sounded pretty good to me. To this day, I recall Maria's theory whenever I watch the back-and-forth rhythm of the waves.

She started kindergarten at our neighborhood public school, Shepherd Elementary. The school was ninety-nine percent African-American and had the devoted support of the area's upper-middle-class parents. Shepherd students ranked first among DC's public elementary schools, year after year.

Kindergarten was a breeze. Mrs. Conniver, Maria's teacher, noticed right away that my daughter was very smart, but also wiggly and easily distracted. To keep law and order in the classroom, Mrs. Conniver awarded stars for good behavior.

"I almost got a star today," Maria reported frequently. "Tomorrow, I know I'm going to get a star," was followed by, "I think I got a star today," and finally, "I got a star today!" I attended my first PTA meeting with great expectations and was therefore shocked to notice that Maria Kreutzer had only two stars, compared to her compatriot Barbara, for example, whose stars circled the classroom. Only one boy with one lonely star trailed Maria's stellar behavior. Sitting still and concentrating in a crowded classroom was clearly difficult for her.

It was Ms. Nickel, Maria's first grade teacher, who noticed toward the end of the academic year that Maria seemed to have problems with reading and writing. I panicked. *What, my smart, creative daughter was deficient?* We started reading out loud. I noticed that she would start a paragraph quite fluently and then begin stumbling, sometimes over words she had just read and now couldn't decipher. Reading was strenuous, and Maria would quickly tire.

"One more paragraph," I'd coax, but she'd feel frustrated and angry and books would fly across the room, reminiscent of our very first attempt at reading. Ms. Nickel recommended that Maria be tested, and that set in motion the district's creaking bureaucracy. It took a year before we got results. Meanwhile, we spent hours at the kitchen table learning to spell short lists of unrelated words, including "window" and "hippopotamus." We practiced until we were blue in the face, and then she still didn't get it right. When I consulted other parents about the difficulty of the task, they shrugged and said that hippopotamus was fun and easy. Looking at the poor results on her spelling tests, Maria started to think of herself as "dumb."

At the end of second grade, we finally received the results of the district's evaluation. A psychologist confirmed that Maria had difficulty with word recognition, spelling, and decoding. We heard the word "dyslexia" for the first time. It's derived from Latin and Greek and means an impairment of the ability to read. In 1987, when Maria was diagnosed, there was little information available on dyslexia. In fact, as of this writing, there is still no single, standardized diagnostic test available. If Maria had been blind, she'd have learned Braille; if she had been deaf, she'd have learned sign language. But since her handicap was invisible, her deficiency in reading and writing was overlooked early and blamed on a lack of concentration.

Today, it is estimated that approximately fifteen percent of the population could be diagnosed as dyslexic. Most of the dyslexic children limp through the public education system and often get diagnosed when they are already well behind their peers.

Maria was eight when the district's report confirmed for the first time that she had a handicap. The psychologist also found that Maria was intellectually superior and actually qualified to participate in programs for gifted children. Tests showed an alarming gap between her verbal and her performance IQ. The district's remedy was to have Maria spend several hours every morning in a special education room. The psychologist mapped out an individualized learning plan with academic goals in reading and writing, and promised to review Maria's progress.

Maria loved Mrs. Brook, her special ed teacher, who always gave "A-plus excellent" for all completed work. There were four others in Maria's group, but their number soon grew to ten—all at different academic levels, often accompanied by considerable behavioral problems. Mrs. Brook had little time for one-on-one teaching, and, when she did, her method of instruction was repetition. Maria bent for hours over mimeographed sheets that needed fill-ins. She'd bring stacks of them home for study during vacations, and I came to hate homework at least as much as Maria did. We'd sit for hours at the kitchen table filling in the blanks, with me alternately cajoling and threatening in hopes of completing a lesson that ultimately brought little learning or enlightenment.

Today we know that dyslexic children have a wide range of abilities and need individualized instruction to address their deficiency. What they have in common is a difficulty breaking words down into sounds or phonemes. The word "dog" is made up of three phonemes, for example, "duh," "ah," and "guh." Most of us understand that, but Maria simply heard "dog" as one sound. When she attended the public school's special education program, she received no help in decoding mysteries like "dog." At the end of third grade, she was further behind in her reading and writing. And by the end of fourth grade, she showed the same test results she had shown the previous year.

"I believe she memorized last year's answers," explained Mrs. Brook, who didn't want to admit total failure in her attempts to educate. Feeling desperate and not knowing any better, I bought her explanation. Maria was so smart that she had memorized last year's test—what a brilliant child! Meanwhile, Maria loathed reading and writing, and her sense of being stupid began to fester.

Mrs. Brook suggested that Maria read for twenty minutes each day. At first I'd sit by her side and fill in the words as she blundered and stumbled:

"Oliver Twist was an—something."

"Orphan," I'd fill in.

She mixed up "then" and "there," couldn't decipher "terrible" or "quickly," finished sentences with "blank-blank," yawned loudly, cleared her throat, and took excessive time to blow her nose. That was followed by "you used my tissue box and now only a few are left," and then a crying fit I tried to cut short with, "I'll get you another box, now stop it!" I was forever pleading for the next paragraph in Dickens' classic tale adapted for young readers. We were miserable, and, when we complained to Mrs. Brook, she suggested that Maria read all by herself. To keep her honest, the door of her room stayed open, the kitchen timer was ticking, and the tape recorder was turned on.

I still have the tape *Maria reads Oliver Twist*, featuring Maria's voice over the ticking of the timer. The sentences are a jumble of "Oliver was going to work—never mind," and "the two boys came to a—whatever." After weeks of this, she informed me triumphantly, "I finished the book, Mummy," and I yelled my hearty congratulations from the kitchen. Listening to the tape now is like reliving a nightmare. Here's this sweet voice trying so hard and succeeding so little. She also cheated mightily, I discovered.

"I still have ten minutes," she says. "I think I'll read another book. Here's one, *The Berenstains' B Book*." That's a preschool book, and I know it wasn't among her pile of options. But Maria commenced with enthusiasm, "Big brown bear, blue bull, beautiful baboon, blowing bubbles …" and ended her reading with a loud "bamm, bamm, bamm!" as if she could blast away all books to kingdom come.

Wendy, the sister of a dear friend, said that she had succeeded in teaching children to read through rhymes and poetry, and, since we were desperate, I asked Wendy to read with Maria on Saturday mornings. Today we know that rhythm and movement can help dyslexics decipher words and sounds, and Wendy's ideas may have been on the right track. But her poems didn't rouse Maria's interest, and the sessions soon deteriorated into acrimony. Luckily, the soccer season started and competed with the Saturday time slot. On the field, Maria was the soccer queen, but in the classroom she felt dumber by the day.

So very smart but feeling dumb

Other cracks in Maria's self-esteem started showing while she attended third grade. Whenever she and Barbara, her Colombian compatriot, volunteered that they were part Indian, kids threw up their arms in mock horror, yelling, "Don't shoot me!"

"We'll need to go to school and give them a lesson on Colombia, Valerie," suggested Janice Grand, Barbara's mother. The girls' enlightened teacher, Mrs. Niedenway, welcomed the idea, and off we went, armed with Colombian coffee and artifacts, and a few simple facts, such as: The District of Columbia and Colombia both take their name from Christopher Columbus; Simon Bolivar, who liberated Colombia from Spanish rule, is called the "George Washington of South America"; and most Colombians are *mestizos*, people of European, Indian, and African ancestry.

We also talked about adoption. Barbara had been adopted as a baby and could show baby pictures; in Maria's earliest photos, she was a toddler.

"But who are your real parents?" the classmates wanted to know.

"I don't know. I was found in a bathroom," Maria volunteered with a shaky voice.

"In a toilet!" screeched a boy, and the whole class collapsed into giggles, with Maria helplessly laughing along.

"That's not funny, that's very sad," Janice interrupted sternly, and Maria's eyes filled as from a hidden spring. She bit her lips to stop their quiver and bravely fought for self-control. I ached for her.

We ended our session by saying proudly who we were. "I'm German-American and I'm proud," I modeled for them.

"I'm Caribbean-American and I'm proud," volunteered the boy who had led the toilet riot. "I'm Colombian-American and I'm proud," said our girls, as, one by one, the children expounded on their mostly African-American heritage. In the end there was just Kelly Kennedy, the only blond, blue-eyed child in class.

"What are you, Kelly?" I asked.

"I think I'm African," she said.

"No, I think you are Irish-American," I suggested since I knew the family.

"Oh, no," Kelly protested, wanting to be like everyone else.

"Come St. Patrick's Day, you might want to go to school and talk to the children about your Irish heritage," I suggested to her father the next time I saw him. He didn't realize that his daughter, in a miniscule minority at Shepherd, suffered from an identity crisis.

"Well, Valerie, we'll just have to do this again next year and the year after and forever," Janice said, as we left the classroom with our Colombian artifacts. We actually did it for two years, and then I received my overseas assignment to Vienna, Austria, where Maria would attend the American International School. Its student body included fifty nationalities. We hoped she'd fit right in.

7.

VIENNA

Before Thanksgiving in 1988, I received my assignment to Vienna as editor of Eastern European editions of *Dialogue*, USIA's flagship magazine. The announcement made me sing and dance with joy. For two years I'd live in my father's hometown, close to my family in Germany, I'd speak my mother tongue, and I'd immerse myself in the culture and history of Eastern Europe.

I had fought hard to get the job. USIA had a small cadre of male editors and designers who shuttled between New Delhi, Tunis, Manila, and Vienna producing exhibits and publications for foreign consumption. It took me a few years to convince Foreign Service personnel that I was qualified to occupy the comfy swivel chair and editorial desk at USIA's Regional Program Office (RPO) in old-town Vienna.

When I broke the news to ten-year-old Maria while we were on the train to New York bound for Thanksgiving with friends, she said she wasn't going. She was well ensconced in her school, the neighborhood, the soccer field, and a circle of friends, thank you very much! Later, when our friends enthusiastically toasted Vienna, Maria balked and didn't lift her glass.

In contrast to Maria, I've always been enthusiastic about relocating and exploring new horizons. I was only four months old when we moved from Berlin's inner city to provincial Schneidemuehl, Pomerania, now in Poland. I can't recall any emotions about that move, of course, but I know from stories that my sisters were ecstatic—also because Papa had promised each a new bike. I was seven in January 1945, when we were fleeing the Russian front at subzero temperatures and lost everything, but that didn't seem to dampen my lust for relocation. After six years in Berlin, my father was transferred to Pforzheim in southern Germany, and I remember poring over maps and brochures to learn as much as possible about the place before getting there. Pforzheim was at the confluence of three rivers and was the northern portal to the Black Forest. The rivers were, alas, mere brooks and disappointments, but the beauty of the Black Forest thrilled me from day one.

I moved to America in a fever pitch of wonder, enjoyed studying and working in different places, including two years in Canada, and then settled in Washington DC for the next seventeen years, acquiring a career, a mortgage, and a child. At USIA, I could observe at close range the effects of Foreign Service life on families, especially the children. Officers moved every two or three years from one place to another, sometimes halfway around the world. Children adjusted, and, when they didn't, they sometime forced their parents to come home. But more often, Foreign Service children turned into world citizens and chose to live in Tokyo or Madrid, to the chagrin of their parents who eventually retired to the DC suburbs and ended up seeing their offspring only infrequently.

I knew instinctively that Maria and I, both immigrants, would do best staying rooted in one place. But the work of my foreign affairs agency was far more exciting in the field than in the DC office, and the assignment to Vienna seemed a dream come true. Maria hated me for it. She had become rebellious lately, and Vienna became as good as any reason to slam the doors, yell "leave me alone," and refuse peace offerings. *What happened to the little girl who thought that we were married?* More and more it looked as if we were headed for divorce.

A breakthrough came when I enrolled in a course based on the teachings of Adlerian psychotherapist Rudolf Dreikurs. The course gave me insight into parent/child dynamics and some ideas for how to rattle my daughter's stubborn streak. Maria gave me lots of opportunities to practice the fine balance between firmness and encouragement, and to skip power struggles in favor of cooperation. I remember one momentous evening in particular.

It was in early spring and a meteor shower had been forecast for that night. We were going to watch it in our backyard. Earlier in the evening, I wanted to share with her the State Department's background notes on Austria. But as soon as she had deciphered the pamphlet's title, she threw it at my feet, ran out of the TV room, and threw herself on her bed.

"Why do you always have to bring it up?" she demanded as I followed her.

"Get out," she yelled. "The door is there!"

"What about this door," I said, moving into the closet.

She got down from her bunk bed and emphatically closed the closet door. I settled on the hardwood floor in the dark. Silence. I could hear Maria busying herself at the table—drawing, I presumed.

"Ha, ha, Mommy is in the closet," she sing-songed.

"Please let me out," I pleaded.

"No," she said firmly.

I stayed in that closet for forty-five minutes, every once in a while pleading with her to let me out. I hoped that she'd open the door she had so firmly closed on me.

"You can turn the knob and get out yourself," she advised.

Finally I did. As I crawled out, I wondered if she'd remember as a grownup how she once held her mother hostage in the closet. We didn't say much as we got dressed for the evening's spectacle of falling stars. It was a cold night and Maria grabbed her snow pants.

"They will be good in Europe," she said pulling them on. I breathed a big sigh of relief.

As it turned out, the city's lights cast an orange glow into the sky that obscured the meteors. We stayed for a while, strained our eyes, and shivered in the cold. We saw no falling stars. They would have been the evening's anti-climax anyway.

We were busy that spring with preparations for departure. I found a management company who found, in turn, a group of yuppie renters for our five-bedroom house. Most of our belongings would be stored, but the piano, a few *kilims* (a type of Middle Eastern rug), some art, and basic dishes were destined for Vienna.

As part of our health assessment, the State Department footed the bill for Maria's educational and psychological evaluation. The battery of tests showed a verbal IQ just below average, but a spectacularly high IQ in the area of visual and spatial problem solving. Her reading and writing ability tested at a second-grade level, though she was in the fourth grade. The Rorschach examination and other psychological tests showed that Maria was sadly lacking in coping skills and was unable to make the compromises necessary to function well socially. The experts recommended that Maria get more help at school and also see a therapist. It was good to have these facts in hand, but also depressing when I realized that we had wasted two precious years in the public school's worthless remedial program. The task of helping this child succeed was daunting.

For now, my own preparations diverted my attention.

I enrolled in State Department seminars on Eastern and Western Europe to learn more about the lay of the land. The Berlin Wall was still intact, and the Iron Curtain ran through the heart of Europe. Speaker after speaker emphasized that the divide made Europe manageable and nobody really wanted the Berlin Wall to fall. A united Germany would be way too powerful, said the department's experts, who preferred the status quo and predicted that the Wall was there to stay. They were proven wrong, of course, when seven months later the Wall came tumbling down. People power had confounded pinstriped predictions.

In June we said farewell to our Washington friends and made them promise to visit us in Vienna. Most of them did. We headed to the airport with two suitcases and a carrier containing our cat, Friskie. The cat had been Maria's idea, and, when we'd first brought him home as a kitten from the pound, Maria had been very playful with him. But as time wore on, Friskie had become my responsibility. Friends had advised that I should take him along to ease the transition into the new home. On my last day, in the midst of an exhausting schedule, I took the cat to the vet for a tranquilizing shot. "That may not work," he warned. "Sometimes it makes them hyper."

And so it did. Stored between our feet on the plane, Friskie kicked up a storm of litter and, mid-Atlantic, released huge stink bombs. With our carrier between us, Maria and I squeezed into the toilet to clean the cage. Once released, Friskie raced around the cubicle, desperate for an escape. But being no Houdini, back he went into the cage.

"Arriving Saturday, 8:30 a.m., Valerie, Maria, and Friskie," I had cabled.

"Is Friskie her husband?" the Austrian secretary had asked.

Mal, a former boss now stationed in Vienna, knew better and placed a litter box and cat food in our new home. By then, Friskie was as exhausted as we were and slept on the king-size bed with us for most of the weekend. He was an outdoor cat and soon explored the vast American compound in the posh neighborhood where we now lived. We had a three-bedroom, two-bath town-home. Our living room opened to the second-floor balcony that gave us a view of tall trees on green lawns. The plunk-plunk of balls from the compound's tennis court punctuated our leisure times.

"When God sends his angels on vacation, he gives them a voucher for Vienna," goes an old local song. I was ready to believe and dragged my doubting Maria on Monday morning to the number thirty-eight trolley that took us to the subway and the Rathaus station in the heart of the old city. From there it was just minutes up the cobble-stoned Schmidgasse to RPO.

The office was housed in a building that dated back to *fin-de-siècle* Viennese grandeur. The central hall's grand, circular, marble staircase was fitted with wrought-iron railings. French doors opened to rooms with twelve-foot ceilings and parquet floors. In the back, a tiled terrace lined with geraniums led into a rose garden with stone benches that were perfect for lunchtime breaks.

Before the war, the building had been a well-known hospital, owned by a group of Jewish doctors. The chief physician and his family had lived in an apartment on the ground floor. After the Nazi annexation of Austria in 1938, the hospital was closed and the doctors were forced to clean the sidewalks with toothbrushes. The chief and his wife committed suicide in their apartment after the first day of this public humiliation.

When the allied tanks rolled into Vienna in 1945, the Americans took possession of the building and turned it into a press and information center. The liberated town's first newspaper was printed on RPO presses. Over the next decades, during the Cold War, the building became the nerve center for publications and exhibits destined for the Soviet Union and communist Eastern Europe. Four American officers supervised a staff of sixty, including translators, photographers, writers, designers, typesetters, and shipping clerks. Many of the local employees came from Eastern Europe, and I had been warned of Balkan warfare right under my nose.

But on arrival, I experienced nothing but Viennese charm.

As I made my rounds, shaking hands to get acquainted, Maria flopped into a leather chair, still groggy from the jetlag. The top designer had the bright idea of printing some stationery with "Maria Consuelo" and the outline of a cat. "Perhaps you want to write to your friends in the States," she said offering the paper. Well, she got no thanks from this child who equated writing with torture. As everyone bent over backwards to please her, Maria remained surly and curled up in her chair. At day's end, my new boss took us to his villa for a lovely evening meal. Maria took one look and said, "I don't eat that," sending our hostess back into the kitchen to scramble eggs.

Maria spent the next few days in the company of an American girl who was a few years older and already city-wise. She introduced Maria to the very easy transportation system of trolleys, buses, and subways. By the end of that week, Maria had visibly perked up and insisted on coming with me to a farewell party for my predecessor on the job. "I'll make you look good," she promised, and I fell for it. At the party, she commented loudly, "You have bad breath," and further mortified me with tall tales of wild parties she liked to frequent. My colleagues smiled with indulgence, engaged her in some clever repartee, and thought that she was quite a pistol. So did I.

Luckily, the American school offered a summer program, which started the following week, and over the weekend we practiced getting there. It meant riding a bus and getting off a few stops before the end of the line. But with her lousy sense of direction, Maria missed the landmarks on Monday and ended up in some vineyards. "There were sticks in the ground with plants around them," she later reported. But she didn't get lost and eventually found her way to school—hallelujah—and actually enjoyed the four weeks of varied indoor and outdoor activities.

Next, we boarded the train for the eight-hour ride to Pforzheim, Germany, so that Maria could attend a Red Cross camp in the Black Forest. She knew the setting from two years before. My sister Heidi and her husband had taken charge of assembling the items on the "what to bring" list. They took Maria and her suitcase to the bus, and periodically checked on her welfare from a few miles away.

The Red Cross ran the camp in a farmhouse in a village. The children helped manage the household by picking up milk and eggs from the farmer in the morning, going shopping in the little grocery store, planning and cooking meals, and cleaning up. During their free time they went swimming and hiking. The girls liked to pick flowers and berries while the boys kicked a soccer ball. Maria soon amazed everyone by joining the boys and scoring well. She also enriched her German vocabulary with a few more expletives.

I had hoped to take a vacation that summer to help us ease into our new life. But my boss said no; mainly, I think, because he wasn't sure whether this first female on the job could deliver. I was determined not to make him regret my appointment and lost no time writing, editing, and commissioning articles for the *Dialogue* inserts. My task was to fill the Hungarian, Czech, Romanian, Bulgarian, and Polish editions of *Dialogue* every two months with sixteen pages of articles of bi-national interest.

For example, when Georg Solti, the Hungarian-born conductor of the Chicago Symphony, was about to retire, we published an article on his illustrious career in *USA*, the Hungarian version of *Dialogue*. And when Betty Guy, a San Francisco watercolorist, took her sketchbook through Romania, we featured her amazing art in *Sinteza*, the Romanian edition of *Dialogue*. For educated Romanians, by the way, our magazine was the only window to the Western world during communist dictator Nicolae Ceausescu's ruthless regime. Every two months, our vans would surreptitiously drop new editions of *Sinteza* at inconspicuous locations. Copies would disappear within minutes to be shared by thousands through a clandestine lending system.

I liked my job and had no problem filling my quota of pages. I enjoyed working with the translators who sat in offices next to mine, and I marveled at our talented designers' artsy layouts. My boss soon reported on my performance to Washington, "She's hit the ground running," and that was the end of our worries. My far more difficult job was to help Maria settle into routines that would help her thrive.

In the fall, she entered fifth grade at the American International School. The school sat on a ten-acre campus next to the famous Vienna Woods and had a reputation for innovative teaching and academic excellence. A third of the school's 800 students were Austrians who, not being part of the diplomatic community, had to pay hefty tuitions. The classes, from kindergarten through the thirteenth grade, were small and occupied a sprawling campus, including a cute cottage that housed the special education teacher. That wonder woman was up to date on all the signs of learning disability, eager to try out new methods, and tireless in her encouragement. Maria went to her cottage at least once a day. In addition, she worked with a tutor twice a week.

As for therapy, I contacted the head of the Adlerian Society in Vienna, who referred me to Dr. Sindefor, a chipper woman with an air of competence. During our first visit to her office, she held up some more Rorschach inkblots for Maria to decipher, and then briefly laid out a series of cards, each containing a drawing. Maria was to memorize the pictures and then pick them out from a group of similar drawings. The test reminded me of the memory games I always flunked. My daughter, however, didn't miss a match. Dr. Sindefor nodded her approval and concluded after fifteen minutes that Maria needed one year of therapy to get over her "minimal cerebral dysfunction."

"Just one year of therapy?" I asked, incredulous.

"Yes," the doctor said.

"And then?"

"Then she'll be fine."

"Wow!"

Maria started right away with Sindefor's young male assistant, Dr. Klupic. I never observed the sessions, but gathered that Maria did rhythmic exercises involving sound and movement. She liked the sessions, which also included little chats on life in general. After only two months, Dr. Klupic told me that he had never had a student who went through the therapy so rapidly. Instead of a year, it would take Maria only six months, he predicted. A nice outlook—also good for my pocketbook.

At the beginning of November, we deserved a break and took advantage of the long Veteran's Day weekend to drive 400 miles to Nuremberg, Germany. Here the U.S. Army maintained a gargantuan PX where the price was right for everything from socks to caviar, and toiletries to VCR recorders, which was a good thing because we now needed a new recorder for European-formatted videos from the lending library. Besides, we needed warmer winter clothes, and Vienna's prices were prohibitive.

The town of Nuremberg is almost 1,000 years old, and still retains remnants of a medieval wall. It is also the home of beautifully restored gothic cathedrals. After supper on our first night, Maria opted to watch American TV in the hotel while I headed for an organ concert at the St. Lorenz Church. Crossing a square, I noticed a group of women and men huddled in a circle holding candles. A sign said that their vigil was in solidarity with the people of Leipzig, East Germany, who were protesting the communist regime with prayers and candles night after night. Tomorrow night I'll join the Nuremberg circle, I vowed, heading for the concert. When I returned to our hotel, Maria shouted, "They've torn down the Berlin Wall!" I was stunned, sank unto my bed, and wept. That night we remained glued to the images of a jubilant people, free at last.

Back home in Vienna, we tried out the new VCR with Shirley Temple movies in preparation for my interview. President George H.W. Bush had appointed Ms. Temple Black as new ambassador to Czechoslovakia, and we needed a profile in *Spektrum*, the Czech version of *Dialogue*. Maria, of course, didn't think much of the 1930s Hollywood productions of charm, dimples, and curly cuteness. But for me, the woman and the Prague excursion became memorable.

I was amazed how tiny Shirley Temple Black looked against the grand French doors of her office in a baroque palace that served as U.S. Embassy. Our meeting was sandwiched between *Good Housekeeping* and *McCall* magazine interviews. Shirley Temple Black's appointment to Czechoslovakia was a media event. By the time I got my turn, her answers were rehearsed and her laughter sounded practiced. When had she first become aware of Czechoslovakia, I asked. "You're the first person to ask me that. Congratulations!" she exclaimed and then recalled receiving a tall Shirley Temple doll in a hand-embroidered folk costume, sent by adoring fans. Many Czechs, including the country's communist dictator, still remembered her fondly as "Shirleyka." That didn't help her when she pleaded for an end to human rights restrictions, including the right to free speech and assembly. During these waning days of the cold war, U.S.–Czech relations had sunk into the deep freeze.

On my flight to Prague, I had sat next to an older man from Israel, invited to witness the fiftieth anniversary of a pro-democracy student uprising that had turned bloody when the invading Nazis put it down. The man's older brother had been among the martyrs, and Prague university students had invited him to participate in a commemoration of the event. "This gathering may turn into a protest against the current regime," my travel companion said. The atmosphere was rife with rumors, but that atmosphere had not yet penetrated our agency's office, where I sat in on a briefing for a *Los Angeles Times* correspondent. He had just witnessed the fall of the Berlin Wall and wondered whether Czechoslovakia's dictatorship would be next to crumble. No, the Czechs were too satisfied with their current way of life, my colleague assured him; developments in Germany would not infect this country.

He was dead wrong, of course. By the time my story went to press, the velvet revolution had overthrown the communist dictatorship. A news agency photo showed playwright Vaclav Havel, the country's new president, hugging Shirleyka, our woman in Prague.

One by one, the dictatorships in Eastern Europe fell like dominoes, and in Vienna we witnessed these thrilling events sitting in first-row comfort. Romania's Nicolae Ceausescu was the last to roll in the dust right after Christmas of that year. We watched the images of his demise with friends from Washington and Bonn. The ancient promise of "peace on earth, goodwill toward mankind" had never rung so true.

Ice skating in Austria

We celebrated the holidays in the idyllic foothills of Austria's Alps. Unfortunately, there was no snow for skiing, but we skated on the lake and hiked up and down the mountains. Maria, who never joined me on my weekend outings, didn't miss a single group activity because the family from Bonn included a dog and three boys, the oldest being sixteen. She marched right in their midst without the usual complaints of "too long" or "too boring." I loved to watch her little bottom in tight jeans as she ascended the steepest inclines, laughing and joking with her newfound friends.

In contrast, our life at home was often marked by bitter warfare. Here's an entry from my diary that year:

"Maria is so angry so often. It's so difficult to live with her. She has no flexibility. She is so stubborn, doesn't want to clean her messy room, bangs the doors, says she doesn't care. I'm so tired of her and of being the adult all the time.

Cheerful thought: Eight more years and it will be over! I'm actually midway, hurrah! I'm the only close person in her life; she doesn't attract any friends. I always have to encourage her to reach out; I have to make the phone calls and arrangements. Part of it may be her LD [learning disability]. I wonder whether it will change as she progresses with her therapy. Sometimes I do see little changes. For example, shopping on Saturday has been great for the past two times. She was really helpful and cooperative."

I remember shopping in Vienna as a nightmare. The stores closed at 6:30 p.m. during the week, at noon on Saturdays, and they stayed closed on Sundays. We did our weekly shopping on Saturday mornings, together with everyone else. The aisles at the crowded supermarket were narrow, and our cart often got stuck as we heaped it with groceries for the coming week. At the checkout, there was no one to bag the groceries—you had to do it yourself. The cashier rang up the items as they rapidly passed by on a conveyor belt. "*Dalli, dalli*, move it," was the norm. I needed Maria's help. She was lackluster at best, and, one Saturday, she just walked away. She wasn't going to help me, she said. "I don't care."

"Okay, no help, no shopping," I said.

On the following Saturday, when I asked her to help me, she said no, so I refused to go. Our supplies in the fridge and cupboard began to dwindle, and, by the end of that week, we were down to a handful of rice and a few pickles. Faced with the prospect of starvation, Maria agreed to come shopping and was a big help.

At school she started to do well academically. She sang in the choir, played saxophone in the band, scored on the soccer field, brought home great art, and earned an A in German. In the summer of 1990, I shipped her off to a pricey computer camp in the Alps, and then put her on a plane to Washington, where our good friends had arranged a four-week schedule of camp, home-stays, and a few weekends in Baltimore with "sister" Rosa. She was in good spirits when she returned home to Vienna, ready to enter sixth grade.

Although Dr. Sindefor had promised to cure Maria's LD, the child continued to struggle with reading, writing, and remembering. In fact, I wasn't sure whether the six-month therapy had made any difference, and I was determined not to fall again for quick fixes. Our struggles at home continued. The disciples of Alfred Adler offered no training program for parents in his hometown, so I reread and underlined my bible, Rudolf Dreikurs's *Children the Challenge*.

We needed help, and I started interviewing male therapists who spoke some English. The scene was pretty bleak. I still get the creeps when I recall a white South African with dubious credentials who practiced hypnosis and pointed to his couch. Hypnosis, he said, was a shortcut to uncovering the evils of the past, and he offered to start with me right then and there. I fled his office. We finally settled on a woman who practiced play therapy with children. Her office was full of toys and possibilities, and Maria didn't mind going there. But, as Maria's belligerence at home increased, I wondered how effective Play-Doh and puzzles were toward ending our warfare. When my visiting sister Claudia asked about sessions with the therapist, Maria said, "I tell her what she wants to hear."

The therapist recommended that I read Alice Miller's *Drama of the Gifted Child*. In this wise book, the Swiss psychotherapist maintains that many of us had to learn as children to hide our feelings, needs, and memories in order to meet our parents' expectations and win their love. Maria's therapist told me to let Maria be and to pursue my own happiness without dragging her along. On Sundays, therefore, I hiked alone through the Vienna Woods or along the Danube, or took the car to explore wine villages. No, Maria would say to my offers to come along, she'd rather stay home. And so I left her in front of the TV in the comfy chair, eating lots of sweets from hidden caches and putting on weight by the pounds. She was surly when I left and angry when I returned, and we spent the evenings often in our separate quarters.

I begged the therapist to add family counseling to her sessions with Maria, but she refused. She didn't want to muddy the "progress" she was making with Maria, she explained. "The hour with Maria is the highlight of my week," she confessed with misty eyes, and I felt tempted to ask if Maria could move in with her.

Our life wasn't relentlessly miserable, however. There were times when Maria was light and happy, especially when we had houseguests. Family members and friends came to enjoy Vienna with the maps, itineraries, and fare cards I would offer on arrival. We had an extra bedroom, so it was easy to accommodate the houseguests—a total of ninety-seven in two years, some staying just a few nights and others for weeks.

In the spring of 1991, Maria stunned me with the casual question, "Do you think you could get an extension of your tour?" It seemed that she had warmed to Vienna's charms. She enjoyed her freedom of movement in the absence of crime, was successful at school, and thrived in art. I, too, would have loved to stay. But the political developments had rendered my job obsolete. As information to Eastern Europe now flowed freely, USIA's magazines lost their *raison d'être* and were phased out. Sadly, we had to say farewell to Vienna.

We were heading back to our big old house on Alaska Avenue and our circle of dear friends. For me, a new assignment was awaiting; and for Maria—heaven help us—a new school.

8.

RE-ENTRY

"Welcome back," I thought bitterly as the cab drove me in the middle of the day from the downtown Washington office to our house on Alaska Avenue. A neighbor had called to tell me that the mailman, who usually traversed our property, had found the side door smashed and boxes strewn all over the yard—a burglary in the middle of the day, perhaps committed by the very people who had moved us back into the house a few days earlier. The burglars had walked off with all of our electronic equipment, including the stereo and computer, one more sobering blow in the re-entry ritual.

July had been hot and muggy with temperatures hovering around one hundred degrees—a big adjustment after Europe's moderate climes. The house needed painting, the air-conditioning needed fixing, the garden was completely overgrown. During those first nights in the half-empty house, I lay awake with a pounding heart calculating the financial and emotional cost of our homecoming. I listened to every creak in our seventy-year-old house, expecting the burglars to strike again any minute. The nation's capital was ridden with crime, buses weren't reliable, the painters didn't turn up as scheduled, and work at the office seemed light-years from where the real action was.

Luckily, I had a few weeks on my own to adjust again to life and work in Washington. Maria had left Europe earlier that summer for camp with best friend Heather. After that she was to spend a week with friends in Boston and four weeks on Cape Cod. Our good neighbors, the Warners, had a summer home at Woods Hole and had invited Maria to be part of their extended family gathering. Grandpa, at almost ninety, was still playing tennis and caused daily anxiety attacks by insisting on driving and then getting lost.

As I worked in my refrigerated office, I received daily telephone bulletins about life on the Cape, including bike trips, swimming adventures, and cookouts. Jane Warner, who had played with and cared for Maria since she was a toddler, also confided that Maria was often withdrawn and spent much time cooped up in her room. She didn't care to join in grocery shopping and other domestic activities. I knew these patterns of behavior, of course, but was surprised and chagrined that they would also crop up in the company of friends. Maria's hosts were concerned about her mood swings and relieved when she would snap out of her sullenness, as she did, for example, when two young adult nieces invited twelve-year-old Maria to come along for an evening of folk dancing. She got dressed in a flash and went off dancing as her perky and chatty self. She loved hanging out with young adults. "Maria could never wait to experience life in real time," a friend observed at the time of Maria's death.

As she charged into adolescence, I wondered if Maria's moody behavior was a rite of passage or a sign of depression. What was a parent to do? Survive the best we can or put her on anti-depressants, as one of Maria's therapists suggested? It occurred to me that the German fairy tale "*Dornröschen* [Sleeping Beauty]" was probably invented by the mother of an adolescent daughter. Why not let her fall asleep at twelve, that ancient mother must have thought, as she spun her tale of wishful thinking, and then have her wake up a hundred years later to Prince Charming or, as a contemporary mother would wish, have her wake up to gainful employment and upright citizenship. I heartily agreed with the message of the tale, especially its happy ending. As it turns out, contemporary adolescents often experience the terrible teens only half awake, doped by illegal or prescribed drugs. Maria never used either, even when she turned runaway and delinquent. Anti-drug messages had been pounded into her brain during childhood, and they had stuck.

At Shepherd Elementary, the glamorous, powerful, and vigilant principal, Mrs. Miller, had hardly let a day go by without warning her students of drugs in the neighborhood. "Yesterday I drove past the 7-Eleven and saw some suspicious activity. I don't want to see any unaccompanied Shepherd student hanging out at that place," she'd announce over the school's intercom. The children, including my daughter, took note. When we ended our week on Fridays by going to the nearby McDonald's for Maria's weekly fix of fastfood, for example, I'd sit watching her inhale her burger, french fries, and milkshake while I looked forward to my veggies back home. I'd be itching to shop for a few necessities at the drugstore next door, but Maria always protested, "No,

Mom, you can't leave me here alone. If Mrs. Miller comes by and sees me, I am in trouble." And so I stayed, expecting Mrs. Miller at any moment.

Our Shepherd era was over by the time we returned from Vienna. Maria's former classmates had graduated, and most of them were headed for Deal Junior High School on the other side of Rock Creek Park. The middle school for our district had a lousy reputation, and savvy parents of Shepherd graduates had cued up in April at the district office for their children's out-of-boundary placement. We had missed the April lineup, while we were still enjoying dumplings in Vienna. I had obtained the name of the Deal principal, and made Maria write him a letter. "I have an LD," she wrote, "but I am working very hard and promise to be a good student at Deal." We never received a response. "I don't think you'll get her in," warned Janice Grand, who had succeeded in registering Barbara.

"Do something, Mom," Maria pleaded. She was dead set on joining best friend Heather and compatriot Barbara, and covered her ears when I mentioned other possibilities. So we went to Deal, ignored the secretary who told us that there was no chance of enrollment, and patiently waited for the busy principal to give us a hearing. "Did you write me that letter from Vienna?" he asked when he finally met with us. He X-rayed Maria with his piercing gaze, and then told his perplexed secretary, "Enroll her!" We were elated.

But not for long. As part of the re-entry process, the State Department footed the bill for another assessment of Maria's intellectual and emotional development. The report was long and alarming.

"Maria is an attractive, friendly, chatty girl who appears very mature," Dr. Parker Wake said in a summary that enumerated Maria's problems at length. "She has problems with writing, listening to directions, and remembering what the teacher said. She seems to forget things a lot, is worried about doing things too quickly without thinking about them, feels she makes careless mistakes, and has trouble keeping her mind on her work. She says teachers confuse her by using hard words and long sentences. She has trouble figuring out how to say what she wants to say in school, and she feels her vocabulary is poorly developed. She gets confused about left and right, has to stop and think about how to make letters and numbers, has trouble copying from the chalkboard, and notes that she sometimes still writes letters and numbers backwards. She finishes her tests late, has trouble with homework, and feels constantly hurried, rushed, and unable to think. She feels that other children are smarter and worries about school and home. She feels that she is not popular, and she gets called names. She prefers to be alone after school. She loses friends easily and finds it hard to make new friends, has trouble finding someone to sit with at lunch, and gets embarrassed easily. On almost every weekend, Maria watches television and video tapes, listens to records and tapes, draws or paints, goes to church, makes bracelets, and feels she is alone. She feels she is excellent at winning arguments."

The psychologist asked Maria to draw a picture of the family. "She showed herself just lying down and mom picking berries. Maria has a deep desire to see her real parents, to know who they are, to get to know her own culture. She wishes her father would come and get her from her new family. She is still very connected to a fantasized past in Bogota."

The Rorschach examination showed that "she is suffering from a serious bout of depression and she is sadly lacking in coping skills. Maria tries to keep her feelings at a distance, controlling them stringently. This is, of course, impossible and can lead to angry, volcanic outbursts. Maria is an angry girl who is having trouble with relationships because she cannot make the compromises necessary to function well socially. She is experiencing enormous demands from her world and she is potentially extraordinarily impulsive."

Academically, Maria was still two years behind in reading and writing, but, since her thinking skills were better than her mechanical skills, she could express herself very well despite poor spelling and sentence structure. Her auditory processing and memory were particularly weak. But she showed excellent attention to visual detail, and superb spatial reasoning skills. "Unfortunately, Maria's strengths are not as relevant to academic success as are the areas in which she is weakest," the testers observed.

They advised monitoring Maria's progress in school carefully and suggested that she might be better placed in a school designed for intellectually capable students with learning disabilities. Maria would not hear of that. They also advised counseling with a male Hispanic therapist.

When I located a male Hispanic therapist after many phone calls, I remembered a social worker joke: How many therapists does it take to change a light bulb? One, but the bulb must be willing. I knew I didn't have a willing bulb.

I accompanied Maria the first few times to the therapist's office at Dupont Circle. She met him with a scowl, and he wasn't sure whether he'd be able to help. The second time they met, he showed her a video about babies who had been separated from their parents. "Tell your mom what we just saw," he coaxed when they returned from the video room. But Maria stayed mute.

It was difficult for me to leave work in the middle of the afternoon to accompany her to the therapist. After a few times, I hoped that she had learned where to get off the subway and find her way. When she didn't turn up for her session it became clear that she lacked motivation more than directions. During a final session with the therapist, I poured out my despair, and he advised me to place Maria in a boarding school. She needed strict structure and supervision, he advised. "I predict that when she is in her late twenties she'll seek therapy," he said, leaving me with a sense of hopelessness since I didn't know how to come up with the $25,000 for boarding school tuition.

Meanwhile, Deal placed Maria with the slowest learners and she saw best friend Heather and former classmates only in the hallways between classes. She was bored and clueless, and her sense of being stupid grew by the hour. I hired Lucie, a brilliant high school student, to come to our house in the afternoon to help Maria with homework. When I returned at six, Lucie had completed her Latin and math while Maria had joked around, distracting Lucie as best she could, all the while insisting that she'd already done homework during recess. When the first Cs and Ds poured in, I hired a professional tutor, the wife of an orthodox rabbi in our neighborhood. Like most adult caregivers, she fell in love with Maria and made it part of her mission to advise her on life in general, and boys and unwanted pregnancies in particular. Academically, her tutoring had little effect.

Maria's special ed teacher in Vienna had suggested checking out Irlen lenses, invented by a California psychologist. News articles credited Irlen lenses with curing dyslexia. In a popular TV show, dyslexic adults who had stuttered their way through a text could suddenly read flawlessly with pink or blue plastic overlays. Still searching for the magic cure, I made an appointment with an Irlen-trained psychologist in our area. She made Maria look at straight lines on a page. Maria saw them as wavy. But with tinted overlays the lines straightened and it seemed that the pastel-colored transparencies also helped Maria to see texts more clearly. I bounced out of the office with elation, but my daughter declared point-blank that she'd never, ever wear pink glasses or use the overlays in school. She desperately wanted to fit into Deal's mainstream.

That seemed increasingly impossible. She brought home low grades and notices of detention for unruly behavior. She started to admit that Deal wasn't the right deal for her, and, by the spring, she was willing to look at the two private schools in the area that specialized in teaching smart kids with learning disabilities. The older and better known of the two, the Lab School, had a waiting list. Chelsea School in Silver Spring, Maryland, had an opening and was only a ten-minute car ride away. When we visited the schools, we were impressed with their rich display of student art. Maria, a very gifted artist, had received a C at Deal for copying the teacher's blackboard drawings imperfectly. At the two alternative schools, colorful creativity enveloped us. *Papier mâché* creatures crowded the admissions office, expressive self-portraits lined the hallways, pottery and sculptures sat on shelves, and murals of jungles and deserts enlivened the staircase. We noticed a different style of learning as we walked along a "history" tunnel, big enough for fourth-graders to crawl through and identify events on a timeline. Doors to classes were open and showed not more than seven students, grouped according to ability rather than age. The curriculum concentrated on developing academic, organizational, and social skills. All students who had graduated from Lab and Chelsea the previous year had gone on to college.

The hitch was the tuition of $15,000, which I didn't have. But a friend, whose son attended Lab, told me how to obtain public funding through legal action. Following her advice, I found my way to the downtown law offices of Bogin & Eig—all marble, leather, glistening glass, and steel. I hadn't gotten much past the towering floral arrangement when an efficient assistant took my data and placed a copy of Maria's recent evaluation into a manila folder. "We'll be in touch," she promised.

To my surprise, Mr. Eig called the next day. "Did you know you've got a genius on your hands?" he asked. No, I hadn't noticed. He said that he had never seen such a huge gap—fifty-five points—between average verbal and very superior performance IQs. "I'm surprised she's still attending school," he said. "This kid needs help. You're lucky that we have two schools here that might be able to help her."

And with that, the lawyers set in motion a six-month process that included assessments, hearings, and observations. The first time the district's representatives came to Maria's classroom at Deal, she happened to be flying toward them in a cluster of boys who yelled, "She started it." They had taunted her about her Colombian origins. "You must be on drugs," they had teased. She had lashed out.

That spring, often skipping classes, Maria discovered joyrides on the subway. There was a bus from our neighborhood to school for a twenty-minute ride. But she could also get there on the subway—the red line connected school and home in a forty-five-minute loop. Like many of her schoolmates, Maria flocked to the subway. Riding through the tunnels and over the city's skyline seemed to give a sense of freedom and flying. She melted into the anonymity of the crowd, pressed into the cocoon of peers, got off when she felt like it, discovered new directions on the yellow and green lines, got lost, and then found her way back. She grinned at cool guys, waved at acquaintances, and felt the thrill of jumping on just as the automatic doors started to close. She crisscrossed the city and soon fell in with a crowd of mostly boys. They'd take over the caboose and laugh when other passengers scrambled for the exit, frightened by the group's boisterous swagger. They began to show off their badness by slashing seats, peeing on the consoles, and scrawling graffiti on the car's pristine walls. I imagine Maria—excited by their daring, perhaps laughing, but also fearful and without a clue how to extricate herself from the mob. The kids' orgy didn't last long; they soon were caught.

Metro police, in their brown uniforms, were waiting for them when they disembarked at the Silver Spring station. They were marched to the end of the platform and asked for their names and school affiliations. "I know you," said one officer, pointing at Maria. "You're a real troublemaker and we're going to get you." He'd never seen her before, but one Hispanic kid seemed to look to him like any other. She cowered. He carried a club and a gun.

Before the day was over, the police complained to Deal administrators, who considered the officer's actions inappropriate and urged parents to register their protest. When I asked Maria about the incident, she swore that she had not participated in the vandalism; she'd just been caught up in it. I was furious. "How dare you threaten my child and single her out without evidence?" I demanded when I spoke to the police officer. He seemed taken aback by this articulate mother of the Hispanic girl. During a long talk, I cooled down and suggested that the problem of vandalism could be appropriately addressed at a school assembly. He was going to consider that. "But how do you get minors to own up to their irresponsible behavior?" he asked rhetorically. It was a question I was to ponder over the next years.

I forbade Maria to ride the subway except for weekend trips to downtown. One Saturday, she asked permission to go to the zoo to meet school friends—a boy and a girl I hadn't met. She promised to be home by nine. When it turned eleven without a phone call, I panicked and called the police. I didn't know the friends' parents, had no contact numbers, and helplessly sat at the kitchen table waiting for a call. Mary, my downstairs tenant and the mother of three grown children, sat with me and brewed a pot of tea, the panacea for all parenting crises. Perhaps they were locked in when the zoo closed, we speculated. Where could three thirteen-year-olds possibly be at midnight? I was shaking with fear when the phone finally rang at one. The mother of the girl informed me that she was on her way to pick up all three. They had been riding the subway until it closed and were now stranded in a Maryland suburb. When I met the group, they were grinning as if they'd just conquered the world. I was relieved to see my child, and hugged her tight. But I was also angry over her disregard for the curfew. I had been beside myself with worry, I told her. "What were you thinking?" I yelled. She shrugged, explained that they'd just had a good time and lost track of the evening. It took me an hour to drive the boy to his home in an upper-middle-class suburb. His father was out of town, he explained, and his mother lived in Korea. His older brother was probably asleep, he said, as we let him out in front of the pitch-black colonial. "Good night," I said. *Good riddance*, I thought.

Maria chose to take her next subway adventure in the middle of an argument. She had to clean up her chaotic room—at least make a dent in it—before she could go out, I had said. It was a Sunday, and I was working in the garden. When I came into the house, she was gone. She called around nine from the platform of a subway station by the sounds of it. She coolly informed me that she'd be home in about an hour. I was furious but also glad; I wanted to rage and cry, plead and threaten. Maria hung up before I could emote. What to do? I called my good friend Marian who always listened well and gave wise counsel. "You have to get tough with her," said Marian. "You can't let her walk all over you." Okay, I'll be tough, I promised.

When Maria called collect an hour later, I didn't accept the charges.

"Why didn't you?" she wondered in a subsequent call. "I guess you'd like me to come home?"

"Of course I do. And you, would you like to come home?"

"No, not really."

"Okay, tomorrow I'll see if you can live somewhere else," I said and hung up, shaking with rage and anxiety.

Shortly after twelve she called to tell me that she was at the Silver Spring station. There was an air of expectation in her voice when she said slowly, "I guess I'll walk home." It would mean a two-mile walk through the barely lit and deserted streets of our residential neighborhood. How often I had come to pick her up! Surely, I would do it now, the voice implied. I didn't. "The house is locked, the alarm is on. You can sleep in the garage," I advised and hung up … and then waited in the darkened house. I sighed with relief when I heard the click of the garden gate. Maria disappeared into the garage and crawled into our red Toyota. I couldn't sleep, and noticed her half an hour later reappearing in the garden. She crouched by the maple tree to pee.

At seven on Monday morning I roused her. "Get ready, I'm driving you to school." I was afraid she'd stay home sleeping all day and then be gone again by the time I returned from work. At the school office, I bought bus tokens and handed them over with a stern warning not to ride the subway.

Being tough felt awful. I asked around for more advice. "I'd rather have her sleep safely under my roof, no matter what," said Janice Grand, who had listened to my story with dismay. I saw her point. So the next time Maria called at midnight from some station platform, I said I'd be there to pick her up, just tell me when and where. My knee-jerk parenting was no match for this child who had decided to whip me for all the disappointments in her life. I teetered in the balancing act between unconditional and tough love, and my angry and frustrated daughter felt nothing but contempt for my parental zigzags.

We did have a few mellow times, especially when she was sick. I fondly remember a week of strep throat that spring when she turned into a sweet and helpless little girl. She wanted me to sit by her bed, feed her chicken broth and pink penicillin, read her a book, and stroke her hot brow with a cool hand.

We had a ritual when she was sick. She'd first crawl into my tidy bed while I pried the door of her room against the floor's knee-deep debris. I'd wash the sheets, and once she was settled back, I'd start to sort the jigsaw of her chaotic creativity. There were colorful pieces of cloth for a quilt in the making; beads half strung for jewelry; shirts twisted in tie-die contortions; multi-colored strings for her lucrative bracelet business; books, tests, sheets with homework half completed; almost a hundred stuffed animals; dirty and clean laundry; crusted plates and cloudy glasses. Cloth, beads, and string were stuck together by glue dripping from a poster project. It usually took me three days before we could see the floor again. I'd bend and pick apart and sort, I'd stack the open shelves along the blue walls, and fold clothes on shelves in the closet where we had gotten rid of hangers because they were too difficult for her to handle. She'd watch, feverish and sleepy, and meekly thank me for restoring order in her universe. "She is so sweet and mellow right now," I wrote to my sister Beate after one such illness, only to add a few days later, "Did I say mellow? As soon as she recovered, she left again. What am I to do?"

But help was on the way. By May, Chelsea accepted Maria, and I was determined that she'd attend, even if it meant getting a second job or playing my guitar on street corners for some change. Chelsea requested that Maria attend summer school, giving our summer some welcome structure. She enjoyed the activities—a mix of reading, writing, and science, framed by soccer, basketball, and roping. "Maria is a real leader," wrote the summer program's director in his evaluation. "I can count on her to help build team spirit."

At a final hearing at the end of July, we won our case for public funding, and, in a spirit of euphoria, we flew off to Costa Rica. The idea for that trip had been born at our kitchen table. She was sick and tired of things German, Maria had complained, as I was preparing supper. "We should be American and Hispanic," she demanded.

"But you are as American as apple pie," I said.

"If I am as American as apple pie, why do I get *Schnitzel* [cutlets] for supper?" she countered. I held the spatula in midair and bent over laughing. But I also realized that her joke obscured a deep yearning for things Hispanic.

"I don't really know who I am," she groaned another time, putting her head on the kitchen table in a gesture of dejection. "I don't even know my language. People talk to me in Spanish and I can't answer."

She hadn't been able to take Spanish at Deal because the program emphasized writing, too confusing for this child who had trouble with English spelling. She had to learn Spanish through the audio-lingual method, and preferably in a program of total immersion. Through a colleague at work, I learned about a former Peace Corps volunteer who had opened a language school in the green hills of Costa Rica near San Jose. I enrolled us and bought plane tickets for this equatorial country.

"This is what your birth country looks like," I told Maria after we landed. It was very early in the morning, and the sun was just rising over the verdant mountains, reminiscent of the landscape surrounding Bogota. She slowly turned and took it all in with a smile of déjà vu. A jeep took us to the village of Santa Ana and our host families. Maria moved in with a family that included two teenagers, while I lodged with a retired social worker just around the corner.

Life in Santa Ana was simple. The only social event, besides neighborly visitations, was evening mass at the cathedral, always packed to overflowing. The villagers knew their liturgies and sang loudly while pigeons cruised above between wooden rafters. After mass, old people huddled for a chat, and young folks in blue jeans sat on the wall that enclosed the churchyard. They laughed, teased, flirted, and paired, until it was time to stumble home through dimly lit neighborhoods.

The rhythm of daily life was dictated by sunrise at five and sunset twelve hours later. Early in the morning, after breakfast, several jeeps gathered the language students for a steep drive up the mountain to the hacienda that had been converted into a language school. The vista from there was spectacular. Layers of green mountain ranges seemed to stretch all the way to the Atlantic Ocean. Instruction took place in rooms with wooden beams or under banana trees. Classes were small; instructors were local and often didn't speak English. Students used their free time to study or nap in frilly hammocks that swayed with the breezes.

I had requested that Maria receive oral instruction only and was happy to see that she quickly bonded with her private tutor, the mother of teenagers. They talked away until lunchtime, when everyone gathered for a main meal, followed by a raucous volleyball game in which Maria excelled competing with the big guys. She was the youngest student and responded to *"Hola, Maria Consuelo!"* greetings with a radiant smile. For once, everyone called her by her full first name, something that North Americans, including her mom, never learned to do.

Seeing her settle in so well, I left Santa Ana to explore Costa Rica via bus and plane. Costa Rica can be easily traversed within a day. The politically stable country did not have an army, but it did have a peace university, and a president who received a Nobel for his efforts to end the war in El Salvador. Between the Atlantic and Pacific oceans lies a wonderland of high mountains with spouting volcanoes, rushing rivers, verdant valleys with lush vegetation, and tropical forests with exotic animals. My well-traveled red backpack soon blended in with those of the younger crowd of devoted eco-tourists who knew where they were headed and generously shared hot travel tips.

When I returned a week later, Maria was holding forth in Spanish with lousy grammar but a native accent. She assured me that she hadn't missed me, and it seemed safe to return to my desk in Washington, leaving my thirteen-year-old for another two weeks with her host family and the school's attentive staff. "I cried when I left," she reported, returning tanned and exuberant with a head of elaborate cornrows and colorful beads. She was determined to return the next year for the whole summer. Wonderful, I said. But when her host family wrote in the spring to remind Maria of her promise to return, the Costa Rica euphoria had fizzled. By then she preferred to practice her Spanish on the streets of Washington's Hispanic neighborhoods.

Returning from Costa Rica with cornrows

9.

INDIAN SUMMER

The yellow school bus started stopping at our house in September, marking the beginning of Maria's academic recovery. She was the last student to board, just a mile and a half from Chelsea. Kids came from a forty-mile radius, and, by the time they reached our house, some had been meandering on the bus for hours. They got used to a longer stop on Alaska Avenue as they watched Maria fly down our steep embankment half dressed.

She usually returned by six after extracurricular activities, including soccer, volleyball, basketball, cheerleading, and student council. She did her homework without prompting, loved math and science, and opined freely in her social studies and history classes. Upon learning, for example, that Henry VIII beheaded his wives because they couldn't produce heirs, she pronounced the king "stupid" at our kitchen table. "Why didn't he adopt?" she demanded. Indeed.

At school, a surprising number of students were adoptees, a phenomenon that has made educators speculate that the children's birth mothers may have had learning disabilities, usually accompanied by impulsive behavior. And, during adolescence, impulsiveness can lead to unwanted pregnancies. To Maria and many of her contemporaries, adoption was a natural process, fit for a king.

During these first months at Chelsea, we breathed easy. Our relationship improved exponentially with every A and every soccer victory she brought home, but my favorite dinnertime was Wednesdays, after her session with Pat McArthur, the school counselor. She'd sit in the kitchen mellowed out, even interested in my day at the office. Years later, Pat told me about her first meeting with Maria. Maria had stood at the door at the appointed time but refused to come in, Pat recalled. "I don't need counseling," Maria advised. "That's all nonsense anyway."

"Well, this time is on your schedule, and you'll just have to stay with me."

"But there is no reason for me to be here," Maria insisted, slowly moving toward the chair to better make her point. Soon she was unloading a tirade of complaints about life in general, and classmates, teachers, and her mom in particular. Pat kept nodding and offering some hints as to how Maria could navigate the minefield of her raw emotions.

"I've never known a child of Maria's age who knows her mind that well," Pat told me during our first conference. "I think I was thirty before I knew my mind that well. You've done an excellent job with her." I bounced away happily that day.

At times, Maria would come up with some amazing insights—like the evening she came into my bedroom and flounced onto my bed. "I think that kids have learning disabilities because they can't remember their beginnings," she said.

"You mean, if they could remember their beginnings, they wouldn't have learning disabilities?"

"Yes."

"Then wouldn't it be better if they tried to remember?"

"Yes. But that's too painful."

We mulled that over in silence.

When the soccer season ended in November, Maria used her first free weekend to visit Rosa in Baltimore. Rosa had graduated from the Maryland Institute of Art that spring. Or had she? There was some uncertainty about that, with Rosa insisting that she had fulfilled the requirements, but the institute saying that she lacked credits and owed money. Maybe she'd hire a lawyer, Rosa had said. Meanwhile, she was looking for a job. Through professional contacts, I had arranged an interview for her at *The Baltimore Sun*. The national editor was interested in meeting her, and I gave Rosa his name and number. Great, Rosa said, but she'd have to assemble her portfolio first. Right now she was working on a stage set for a Christmas ballet. It had been described as small and simple for an easy $200, but it took longer than expected and she was slaving away day and night. She was living with tall and blond David who was working in his family's local construction business. Their apartment was a work in progress. The bedroom had been dismantled down to the studs, and there was a big hole in the bathroom that was to be filled with a sunken tub. For Maria, Rosa was an exciting role model. She, too, would study art, just like Rosa, she said. The squalor of Rosa's Bohemian lifestyle looked exotic. Maria returned from the weekend with artsy black-and-white photos that showed the "sisters" clowning around Baltimore's harbor. Rosa had developed the pictures in her dark room.

Before going away for the weekend, Maria made sure that she wouldn't miss too much sex at Sunday school. Our Unitarian church offered her age group a course on human sexuality with a curriculum that had been developed decades ago. With help from filmstrips and videos, the man-and-woman teaching team discussed anything and everything, from the pervasive sex appeal in advertisements to the scourge of transmitted diseases. The 22,000-piece AIDS quilt had just been spread out on Washington's Mall, and the names of 160,000 victims had been read during three days of solemn commemoration that included candlelit vigils in front of the Clinton White House.

At Sunday school, however, things were kept light and lively. The class was so popular that kids, for once, begged their parents to take them to church lest they miss a Sunday. "We're laughing our heads off," Maria reported. When they practiced putting condoms on cucumbers, for example, a boy said that he'd rather practice for real. Ha, ha, laughed the group, "Yours is way too small!" And so it went, with plenty of discussion on responsible and safe sex. After a weekend retreat and a visit to Planned Parenthood, Maria had a starter set of condoms in a basket on her bookshelf. Over the next years, it grew into an international collection, keeping her virginity intact—as far as I knew.

"We've survived another year of adolescence," I wrote to friends in my Christmas letter that year. "There are times when I want to put a sign on Maria's room: Checkout Time June 1997. But then there are times when she delights me with a bewitching poem or an A in math, cracks me up with her quick wit or demonstrations of the latest dance moves, and impresses me with her athletic and artistic excellence."

Clowning at Christmas

That Christmas we celebrated in grand style. "Are you sure you transported that tree in your Toyota?" marveled my friend Katie who joined us on the fourth of Advent for our traditional carols, cookies, and supper. My mother's handmade straw stars covered the nine-foot spruce, and candles lit the whole house. As guests pushed little presents under the tree, Maria and her friend Heather kept diving under to investigate, making the tree tilt just as we were into "Silent Night."

Some of our friends had been caroling with us for decades. When Maria arrived on the scene shortly before Christmas in 1980, we didn't have a tree, and the cookies came from the store, but our friends gathered in time for carols. Maria sat in diapers next to me on the piano bench, pounding the lower keys with gusto, almost drowning out "Joy to the World." This year, along with her longtime friend Heather and Heather's mother, Ellen, she had invited Carl, a new friend from Chelsea. His mother, who played the recorder, joined us, and an intern at my office brought her violin. In case of any glitches, Ellen's brilliant and strong soprano always carried the tune and added rhythm to "Go, Tell it on the Mountain." We must have sounded pretty good, because a latecomer reported that cars were stopped in front of our house, and drivers were listening for a while through rolled-down windows.

In a letter to my three sisters, I mused about the origins of our holiday traditions.

"Remember Mutti's cookie productions?" I wrote. During the lean war years, my mother started in the summer saving ingredients for the dough she would roll out in December. In my earliest memories, I kneel on a kitchen chair to help her cut out angels, stars, and circles. Mutti let us taste the dough and the first batch of baked cookies before she stored the rest of them in tins for Christmas.

In Germany, Christmas Eve is the holiest night of all festivities. My father usually put up the tree in secrecy earlier in the day. We prepared for the evening by bathing and dressing in our best. While Mutti was busy spreading gifts under the tree and cooking supper, Papa was tasked with entertaining us. If there was snow, he took us tobogganing at a hilly nearby park. He made us assemble like organ pipes onto a way-too-short sled and then steered us down the steepest slopes. Inevitably, we'd careen into the deepest drifts, with all of us piling into a gigantic snowball. Like fathers of his generation, he wasn't the hugging type, and these rough-and-tumble wrecks were his idea of familial closeness. As we'd disentangle from the pile, Papa would brush snow from his coat and hat with hearty laughter, while I cried. Sitting up front, I got the brunt of snowy tumbles and was glad when we were heading back home.

A bell announced the magic moment when the French doors to the dining room opened, revealing a tall, candle-lit tree in the corner by the window. It was decorated with silver tinsel and shiny balls, and so awesome that we approached it with the reverence the kings and shepherds must have felt in Bethlehem. Papa, all recovered from previous frolics, and pastor once again, read the chapter from Luke. That was followed by all verses of *"Oh, du fröhliche"* and *"Stille Nacht,"* solemn songs of wonder and mystery sung a cappella in harmonies. By the time we hit the last chord, we had usually figured out who would get the knitted mittens or socks or woolen scarf lying unwrapped under the tree. Papa distributed the gifts, everyone got a plate of cookies and sweets, and then Mutti topped it off with a scrumptious meal. The doors to the living room and study were wide open, and the tiled corner stoves were, for once, roaring at full blast. We felt warm and happy.

At Christmas in 1944, we could hear the distant thunder of the war's approaching front, and our parents' mounting anxiety muffled our celebration. Shortly after Christmas, we fled the onslaught of the Russian army, barely escaping with our lives as our home went up in flames. Thereafter, Christmas was never the same. But from the yarn of Schneidemuehl memories, we each have spun traditions of our own.

"Now is the time to start your holiday traditions with Maria," admonished my oldest sister when we were headed for our second Christmas. "Make it a festive evening," Beate advised. "Put Maria in a pretty dress, ring the bell, sing a few songs."

"Give me a break," I thought that evening as I was heading home from work. In addition to my briefcase, I carried Pampers and a few hastily bought groceries. "No," I told Maria, who was trudging beside me in her yellow snowsuit, "I can't carry you. You have to walk." But she refused and threw herself in practiced fashion onto the icy sidewalk. That was it! I roughly pulled her up, smacked her padded bottom, and, ignoring screaming protestations, marched her home. As soon as the door of our apartment had closed, I dropped my child and bags and collapsed. I felt overwhelmed by the discrepancy between how our Christmas Eve ought to be and how it really was. Maria, almost three, forgot her own laments and watched my sobs with interest. When I reached out to her and said that I was sorry, she refused to let me touch her, making me cry harder. She went to the bathroom and returned with a box of Kleenex, which she shoved into my face. I accepted the peace offering, and we survived the rest of that evening in friendly compatibility, though without bells, dresses, or songs.

As she grew older and I more organized, we developed some Christmas Eve traditions that included a group of intimate friends. They'd come for supper and slip their presents under our tree. Maria would outline the evening's events in a program—I still have the one from 1992.

On the green cover she wrote in her typical in-charge style, "CHRISTMAS by Maria Consuelo Kreutzer-Mendez," and then listed inside:

> Drinks
> Stereo Gift to Maria Consuelo
> Dinner in dining room
> Letter from a Friend, read by Lois
> *January* (poem), read by Maria Consuelo
> *A Child's Christmas in Wales* by Dylan Thomas, read by all
> Gifts for all
> Dessert for all
> Merry Christmas to All!

That Christmas, Maria got a coveted boom box so we could have music during dinner, since I hadn't yet replaced our stolen stereo. But the evening's climax was our readings in front of the fireplace. Over a fifteen-year period, we covered all the Christmas classics, starting with the Bible and Dickens, and then unearthing chapters in novels that touched on the holiday. Our search for literary jewels was year round and had an edge of competition. On Christmas Eve, we shared our finds by passing books around the circle. As soon as she could read, Maria loved to take her turn, and everyone listened to her starts and stumbles with patience and encouragement.

Then Maria would retrieve gifts from under the tree, one by one. We watched Marian unpack a present from her sister, admired the jewelry Sam gave to Nancy, and appreciated the little presents we had for each other. Maria, of course, got the lion's share and went to bed a happy camper.

As soon as the last Christmas decoration was stored in the attic, the universe and our household prepared for her birthday at the end of January. When I look at birthday photos, I realize that we usually had more than one celebration—one with kids and a few more with adult friends and neighbors. Maria always took charge of the decorations and converted our downstairs into a crepe-papered Shangri-La. For her fourteenth birthday, she invited Carl and three other classmates from Chelsea, the first time in three years that she had friends to invite. Pat McArthur helped her think about how the afternoon should be. Maria's birthday program included a soccer match on the grounds of the nearby elementary school, and Twister, a game that gets you onto all fours with contorted arms and legs, often around each other in ever new and exciting poses. All went well with lots of giggles. I kept a low profile in the kitchen and appeared only to cater fizzy juices, a store-bought cake with soccer symbols, and homemade lasagna for the evening meal. "I didn't even mind that you were around," Maria said when the guests had left, and I took it as a compliment.

She wasn't always that benevolent. There were times when she said that she couldn't spend another night under the same roof with me, and sometimes best friend Heather's mother, Ellen, took her in to give us a break.

"Teenagers!" exclaimed Rosa who often had to listen to my motherly frustrations. "She's a teenager, Valerie! Just ignore it," was her advice.

Living with my teenager also had its lighter moments, like the time she was raising mice without my knowledge or permission in her messy room. She had casually asked me for a box. "About that big," she had said, vaguely outlining the circumference of something pretty big. She needed the box for a project. Obligingly, I looked in the garage, the basement, and the attic, and —voilà—would this do? "Yes, perfect," she'd said. "Many thanks." And then had disappeared into her room.

That chaotic room had been a bone of contention for many years. But after threatening, cajoling, bribing, and scolding to no avail, and, after some parenting courses that preached the art of letting go, we had arrived at a truce: You pick up your stuff in the rest of the house, but in your own room you can live as you wish, as long as no vermin escape to the rest of the house!

I forgot about that box. Her innocent question as to what mice might like to eat, and then looking for cheese in the fridge, should have tipped me off—but didn't—until one late evening, while crawling upstairs to my bedroom, I tripped over a white mouse escaping from Maria's room. As if on cue, I let out my primal scream and pushed against the debris in her room, only to discover that my box was inhabited by a colony of white mice. "Out," I roared. "Ha, ha, ha," Maria responded, collapsing onto the pile of dirty laundry on her bed. She had been waiting for my outrage, and grinned with glee. The mice, she explained, had come from school and were supposed to live happily in the box left open for air. But the creatures were now too big and taking over. Sorry about that. "Out," I continued to yell, and, after further tedious negotiations in which I probably lost ground on more important issues, I prevailed, and the mice were chased out of their comfy habitat into the cruel wider world. The last I saw of them was a white flicker over the fence with Magic, our vigilant retriever, giving them a barking send-off. "How about some snakes?" she suggested next. "Not in my house," I said.

I had grown up without pets. During and after the war we had no extra food to feed a pet. We were as poor as the proverbial church mouse, but field mice often found their way into the kitchen pantry of our drafty parish. My mother, a country girl at heart, caught and chased them fearlessly and once squished one with a broomstick in the corner of my room when I lay sick in bed. I barely recovered. All my sisters and I ever did was scream at the sight of mice, while my mother kept the upper hand. But when she was gone for one reason or another, the mice took over, and Papa barely noticed our plague. To this day, if you mention mice to the Kreutzer sisters, you will see our hair stand on end.

Whenever Maria said that she needed a pet, I postponed discussions and action as long as I could. First we got Friskie the cat from the pound. Then, after our break-in, everyone including the police advised us to get a dog, so we adopted Magic. Maria helped pick her out in the pound and swore she'd take care of her. And, for about ten days she actually did. But after that it was my job to walk, feed, and take the dog to the vet. Inevitably, I fell in love with Magic and looked forward to our daily walks, come rain or shine. When I returned from work, Magic jumped for joy and raced around me as if to say, "I've missed you all day, I'm so glad you're home." Maria, in contrast, barely acknowledged my return with a grumbled, "Leave me alone."

At school, however, Maria was thriving. "Last year I could only dream of such grades," she marveled when she made honor roll that spring. For her community service requirement, she had started volunteering at Barbara Chambers, her old preschool. During her three years there, the school had been socially and economically integrated. Since then, public funding had turned it into a center for Hispanic children from low-income and Welfare families. Maria thus got to know a new slice of life. On Wednesday afternoons she had five toddlers under her care. She talked to them in Spanish and administered lots of *abrazos* [hugs]. "We have to give them a lot of love because they don't get much at home," she reported. Paulette, the director, was thrilled to have Maria back, and promised a summer job if extra funding should become available. At fourteen, Maria was eligible for the mayor's summer employment program, and we signed her up. One of the proposed projects was painting murals on public buildings—a perfect job for this budding artist.

At work I seized the opportunity to do temporary duty in New Delhi in June when local temperatures there soar to 120 degrees and everyone in their right mind flees the city. I would be sitting—albeit clueless—in the press attaché's leather chair, supervising a staff of Indian information specialists who would assist me in analyzing and reporting the latest wrinkles in Indo-U.S. relations.

In preparation for our six-week separation half a world apart, I asked Rosa if she'd be interested in moving into our house to look after Maria. Yes, she said, she was very interested since she wanted to separate from longtime boyfriend David. She had a new budding relationship with some Eric who wanted to marry her. She was thinking of moving back to DC to find work.

Staying with Maria during the summer would suit her needs, she said, and Maria was ecstatic over that possibility.

Next I had a call from David.

"I'm very concerned about Rosa," he said. "She's into drugs. It's really bad. Can you help?" I had met David a few times, but never for longer than a handshake. Now he counted on me as an ally. He had read stories of how friends gather and forcibly take an addict to a rehab center. He wanted me to show up very early some morning at Rosa's bedside and help him commit her to an institution. I was dumbfounded and said that I needed to talk to Rosa first. When I called and told her of David's concerns, she laughed outrageously.

"He's the one who's into drugs, Valerie," she insisted. "He's out of his mind. Trust me!" I always had, and promised that I would. As for her stay at the house in my absence, she wasn't so sure right now. So I started looking for another *au pair* and found Rita, daughter of our dear downstairs neighbor Mary.

Rita had just graduated from college and was taking time off to contemplate the direction of further graduate studies. She was competent, headstrong, and the survivor of a troubled adolescence. Though Rita and Maria gravitated toward each other, I wasn't sure if the chemistry was right. But Mary would keep a motherly eye on the pair. Rita would receive an *au pair* salary, funds for weekly grocery shopping, and hand Maria a weekly allowance. When Rosa called at the last minute and said that she'd be available, after all, I told her that I'd already hired Rita, but Rosa could certainly stay at our four-bedroom house during her transition. With confidence, I kissed my child good-bye and told Mary how grateful I was for her generous support. She waited with me for the taxi to the airport.

I arrived in New Delhi at midnight, India's magic hour because the modern nation was born in 1947 at the stroke of twelve. The ride through the capital was eerie. Tree-lined, broad boulevards were almost deserted, except for occasional groups of grazing or sleeping cows and hordes of scrambling monkeys. Minarets of temples and silhouettes of colossal buildings were dimly lit and looked familiar from having watched *Jewel in the Crown*, a Masterpiece Theatre series about Britain's loss of the subcontinent.

The air-conditioned embassy car kept the brutal onslaught of the heat at bay and delivered me to the spacious apartment of a colleague who was on home leave. The four-bedroom apartment came complete with Mr. Kumar, an experienced servant who lived on the American compound and supervised a gardener, and the cleaning staff. Mr. Kumar soon became my best friend. He knew of diets and mixtures when I got sick, worried until I got better, and beamed when I told him that I'd never had it so good.

The taxi ride on my first morning was a hair-raising experience of near misses and miraculous escapes. Motor scooters and three-wheel taxis dominated, often carrying the extended family. Buses were overcrowded; poorly paid and inexperienced drivers caused daily accidents and fatalities—"And Now Killer Buses," a *Washington Post* headline screamed.

The American Center, my workplace, was a five-story building in a busy downtown section, next to the daily *Times of India*, and down the street from the elegant British High Commission and the busy German cultural center. The most frequented part of the American Center was its library, whose 30,000 patrons showed up especially during the hottest months, if only for its reliable air-conditioning. The place was packed, and the librarian who showed me around casually introduced me to a well-known poet here, and an outstanding scholar there, doing their research, penning deep thoughts, while students watched videos in carrels.

The routine of my days was soon established. I began by reading wireless news, scanning the previous night's TV reports, and reading eight Delhi papers. At around 9:15 a.m., six press assistants filed into my office and briefed me on Indo-U.S. relations as reported in the regional Urdu and Hindu press. We prepared daily and weekly briefings for key officers at the embassy and in Washington, and fielded inquiries from U.S. and Indian news organizations.

I loved the work and felt productive. I enjoyed the camaraderie among the Americans, with little dinner parties during the week and shopping sprees to favorite bazaars on weekends. Though I wilted in the heat and returned with fever and diarrhea from my outing to the Taj Mahal, I tried to absorb as much as possible of India's atmosphere. It's a popping land, with a population that grew by one million in the four weeks I was there. Even the dullest person, it seemed to me, couldn't help but feel stimulated by the splendor of India's past and the enormity of its challenges in the present.

On Sunday mornings, I met some colleagues for brunch at the embassy's American Club and then drove with them to Mother Teresa's orphanage clear across town. There we cuddled babies for a few hours: emaciated newborns, crippled infants, chubby cherubs, and sad and listless toddlers—about seventy-five of them. I remembered petitioning Mother Teresa for a child fifteen years earlier. She had turned me down because I was single and not Catholic. I took photos at Mother Teresa's and later showed them to my staff. The Indians were amazed. This was the cultural attaché cuddling a dark-skinned orphan boy? And here the junior officer taught a crippled child to crawl? For my Indian colleagues, these orphans were "untouchables," and I realized that old prejudices still prevailed, despite Gandhi's courageous and relentless barefoot crusade against hatred.

When I called Maria on weekends, I usually got a sleepy and mellow, "Hi, Mom!" Finals had been tough, she reported, but she got ninety-eight in math. Rita was okay and Rosa was in and out. But the curfew of 10:00 p.m. was way too early, she complained. Too bad, I said, amazed that I still had some clout halfway round the world.

During the next phone call, Maria was crying. She had injured her knee again at soccer, the second injury since May. The knee had been X-rayed at Children's Hospital, but the diagnosis was vague. She had been given a brace and painkillers and was hobbling around on crutches. She wouldn't be able to work this summer and wondered what to do. Summer school was a good option, we decided. As for the home scene, Maria was bitter about her piddling allowance. "Rosa and I want to go out but we don't have any money," she wailed, "Rita is so mean and stingy." I got the impression that the *ménage à trois* wasn't working.

"Let them be," my sister Beate advised when I stopped in the Black Forest on my way back. "Rita is in charge and they'll just have to figure things out." I took her advice and pretended that I was as free as the breezes as I bicycled along the Murg, a mountain river. I relished the crisp air, lush meadows, and tall evergreens of the enchanting landscape, and I indulged in the warmth of my family's embrace.

"Mammy, Mammy," Maria cried out, hopping toward me on one leg when I returned. I hadn't arrived a minute too soon, it turned out.

Washington was in the grip of a heat wave and our air-conditioner wasn't working. My car's battery was dead. The house and garden looked neglected. Rita had retreated to the apartment downstairs and didn't care to talk to me. Rosa was at large. Magic had stopped barking.

Bit by bit, I learned about life in my absence. Early on, Rita and Maria had their disagreements, and, after Rita's mother had left for a trip, Rita sought advice from our good friend Ellen who did her best to mediate. She and daughter Heather actually sought refuge in our house while their house on Taylor Avenue was fumigated after their cats' case of fleas. Up close, Ellen observed that Maria and Rosa had formed a united front against Rita, who held the power and the purse. Rosa's fiancé, Eric, visited often and befriended Maria, while Rita's boyfriend moved in and settled next to her on my futon. Maria more or less took care of herself, though our good friends looked out for her. Lois made sure she attended summer school, Judy took her along for a weekend at the beach, and good friends from Boston stopped by to visit. But I had been missed.

Within days, I had the car and air-conditioning running, tidied house and garden, put flowers on the kitchen table, and cooked square meals. Maria went to physical therapy, and, when that didn't help, the sports medicine doctor advised surgery. In August, she had an arthroscopy to be followed by more therapy. She was brave throughout, and a photo from the day of surgery shows her bedraggled but smiling while sitting on my bed with a heavily bandaged leg. As usual, she was the sweetest and most cooperative patient, and she even thanked me for cleaning out her room. We rounded out that endless summer with a two-week vacation driving up the coast, seeing friends along the way, and then attending a Unitarian family conference on Star Island, off the coast of Portland, Maine.

In my memory, the Star Island week is framed in bliss. Rocking on the porch, I sat for hours watching glorious sunsets, or storms whipping up the waves. For further distraction, I could choose lectures and workshops on anything from arts to politics. In the evenings, we lined up for quiet ascents to the two-hundred-year-old chapel, where we hung our lanterns on hooks to shed light on contemplative services. Maria, meanwhile, hung out with high schoolers and roamed the rocky island into the wee hours of the morning. She was happily ensconced in her peer group, produced some fabulous art, and acknowledged my presence with little waves from afar. She was teary when the boat returned us to the mainland and vowed to return next year and every year thereafter—another pledge she soon forgot.

As school started in September, it looked as if we were back to normal, though remnants of the Indian summer remained. I had tried to meet with Rosa, but she had moved back to David in Baltimore, according to Maria, who kept in touch with Eric and his friends. She was secretive about these contacts and talked on the phone at all hours of the night. Whenever I answered, the callers hung up. Once, Eric was on the phone at one in the morning and apologized for calling so late. He had just returned from Venezuela, he said. In his job as engineer he traveled a lot, he explained. He needed to get in touch with Rosa and asked if I had her address and number. No, I didn't, I said, but would he please come and pick up his black leather coat, which still hung in our closet. He promised he would.

That coat remained an odious reminder of the chaos that had reigned in my absence. It was brand new, still carried its sales tag, and permeated the whole downstairs with a leathery smell of newness. I wanted it gone. I wanted all signs of weird comings and goings in my house to disappear. For the next few weeks, the coat wrapped Maria into single-minded attempts at delivery. Eric would call and promise to stop by to pick it up. He'd come in a gray Mercedes, he said one time, in a green Cadillac the next. And Maria would sit and wait on our front steps until nightfall.

Could she meet him at Union Station? he asked the next time he called, and dutifully Maria headed with the coat toward the old train station that had been converted into a swinging mall. Hours later she called because Eric wasn't where he had promised to be. It was getting late, and I was concerned. Ellen and Heather had stopped by and offered to drive with me to the station.

We entered the grand, marble-tiled hall looking for Maria and decided to split for our search. And then I saw her, talking excitedly to a skinny, short guy in his forties, wearing "the" black leather coat. When I approached, he sheepishly hid a beer under the coat's flap as my child's charmed expression turned into cold hostility.

"Eric," I said firmly, "I am Maria's mother, and, now that you have your coat, I want you to leave us alone. Don't ever call again! And Maria, you come home with me right now."

"No, I'm staying," she said, quickly moving toward the busy mall. Just then Ellen and Heather approached and stepped into her way.

"You get your little butt into your mother's car, girlfriend," Ellen demanded with authority. "You are lucky that you have a mom who loves you and cares about you and keeps you off the streets. You get into her car right now!"

And Maria did. On our way home, she unleashed a barrage of rage. I had no right to butt into her relationships, she said. She couldn't wait to be rid of me and live her own life. I ruined all the fun she ever had and embarrassed her in front of her friends. She hated me, she screamed. White-knuckled, I held on to the steering wheel. Thanks to Ellen, I was able to ferry my fourteen-year-old to the safety of home. But lying in bed that night, I cringed under the wave of hatred emanating from my daughter's room.

Maria continued making long-distance calls, using a beeper and a number Eric had provided. During an outing, she confided to our friend Sandra—who immediately reported back to me—that she owed Eric, who had had to pay $200 to someone who associated Maria with a drug deal gone bad. I was horrified, but, when I asked about her dealings with Eric, she immediately clammed up. One day, when I was off work and Maria was at school, I searched her room and found an opened letter addressed to Rosa. It was from Eric, who swore his undying love for Rosa in the illiterate scribbles of a six-year-old. The envelope contained some rusty keys—to his heart, his house, and his yacht, as Eric wanted Rosa to know. I put it all into an envelope with a note to Rosa: "You should know that your connections have brought great anxieties into my life," I wrote. "According to Eric, David is a known drug dealer who has you hooked on drugs. I wonder what has happened to you. Please contact me."

The envelope was returned as "undeliverable." But Rosa called me at work shortly thereafter. "Valerie," she said with desperation in her voice, "You must get Maria away from Eric and his friends. They are terrible people. They are after me; I had to leave my place. I'm in hiding."

"Please tell me where you are," I pleaded, "I want to see you. Perhaps I can help."

"No, I can't tell you where I am. But I'll be in touch. Good-bye."

I never heard from her again, and had no way to find her. For twelve years, Rosa had been part of our family—Maria's big sister, my other daughter. And then she was gone, leaving us with shattered dreams. I felt bereft.

10.

RITES OF PASSAGE

That fall, Maria's age group started the course that would lead to rites of passage at All Souls, our downtown Unitarian church. The ceremony is the equivalent of confirmation or *bar/bat mitzvah* in other faith traditions. At the onset of the year, adolescents choose mentors from the congregation, and Maria asked effervescent Dolores, who had also guided her through the sexuality curriculum, to be her mentor. Dolores said she was flattered.

A single parent of a teen, Dolores juggled her busy schedule to make room for Maria. They went to movies and the mall, took walks, and had long talks in which Maria told tall tales but also confided secrets of her head and heart.

During the course of the year, the fourteen youngsters in her group would explore their religious and spiritual beliefs and climb into the pulpit one by one to read, dance, sing, or drum their statements of faith and affirmation.

Maria was a few months into the exercise when it occurred to her that she was actually Catholic. I had told her early on that she had been born Catholic and had probably been baptized Catholic in accordance with the customs of her birth country. Now that she was about to define beliefs based on Unitarian principles, she claimed to be Catholic. It felt like another venue of rebellion around the chalice on our kitchen table.

I swallowed hard and then suggested that she practice her faith by attending mass with our downstairs neighbor Mary, who walked across the street to the Walter Reed chapel on Sunday mornings. Maria also had to tell Dolores about her change of heart, I insisted.

"I accept your decision to drop out," said Dolores, "but I'm sad because you deprive me of the pleasure of being your mentor." Maria quoted Dolores with a little smug shrug. For a few Sundays she joined Mary at mass in the grey field stone chapel with its red doors. The elderly women congregants happily fussed over this born-again Catholic and stuffed her with extra donuts during coffee hour. The priest smiled on her and wondered how to involve Maria in the service. Would she like to sing a solo perhaps? How about the Spanish folksong "*De Colores*"? For a week or so Maria warbled, "*De colores se visten los campos en la primavera* … [All the flowers we see in the country in springtime …]," as printed in our Unitarian hymnal.

But warbling, kneeling, and blessings aside, she missed Dolores and the laughter and heated arguments with the kids at church school. I tried to keep my elation in check when Maria announced that she'd complete the rights of passage year after all. She advised us of her decision with this air of I'm actually Catholic but will go along with Unitarian nonsense for just one more year—aren't you thrilled!

And I was.

For her year-end statement, Maria chose to ponder the question, "Do I believe in God?" She interviewed her peers and Dolores on the subject and consulted books from our shelves. "To believe in God is to get high on love, enough to look down at your loneliness and forget it forever," she quoted one author who also said, "To believe in God is to know that all our stars are lucky ones." But a friend, Maria reported, said, "I don't believe in God. Sometimes I pray but nothing happens. So there is no proof that there is a God. If there is a God, why are there so many homeless people, diseases, wars, and hate?"

Maria also quoted "a grownup friend"—was it Dolores?—"I was brought up and told there is a God and I must believe in him. I came to a point in my life where I questioned what I had been told about this very strict male God. Over the years I came to the conclusion that there is a God-force, which I believe in and rely on very strongly. This loving God I call Mother-Father-God."

Maria concluded: "I don't believe in one of these quotes, I believe in a part of all of these quotes. I believe God is all around you, and he is your heart and soul."

She had started wearing a small golden cross on a necklace and wore it to her dying day. When Natasha searched the wreck after the accident, she found on the car's floor Maria's cross, torn from its delicate chain.

"For a kid her age, Maria was amazingly serious during rites of passage," observed a church and family friend, who remembered Maria during the memorial service at All Souls. He saw Maria's struggle with her Catholic heritage as part of her adoption odyssey. "The best time was when Maria had worked through a lot of her stuff and would come bouncing into church and hug me with the biggest smile. She had all this energy and love to share."

"She never hesitated to speak her mind," remembered Maria's church school teacher. "She expressed enlightened views, often ending with 'but I'm a Catholic, not a Unitarian.' So I said, 'Well, Catholics are welcome here.' And this went on for several years. But when I asked her at the reception for high school seniors how things were, she said quietly, 'I think I'm a Unitarian after all.'"

But, at fifteen, she was in the midst of a religious muddle. In the booklet that introduced the fourteen candidates, Maria Kreutzer-Mendez stated:

"Because of my religion, Catholic, I try to forgive and not make the wrong choices. I think religion is a very big influence on me sometimes. I think, 'What would the minister or priest say if he saw me do some of the things I do?' So I try to do right. It also gives me many things to think about and to compare my religion to others. Religion has also influenced my morals and standards."

Maria's was the longest ramble. The others, including a political refugee, just off a life raft from Haiti, echoed principles of tolerance. "Religion has helped me accept other people of many cultures," wrote the young Haitian. And Harvard-bound Michael said, "Being a Unitarian Universalist means that I don't have to believe in any being or higher intelligence, such as God or aliens. It also means that I respect people, no matter what they believe in, even if I think it is crazy."

There were lighter times before this confessional finale. Like the Saturday when the kids carried sleeping bags into the church basement for a night of bonding. They cooked supper, talked, and played past midnight, and, after lights went out, kept joking and giggled, especially over one mentor's resonant snores.

They say that it takes a village to raise a child, and, on that Sunday in the spring of 1994, the villagers assembled at All Souls to acknowledge our youth's passage from childhood into adolescence. It was a solemn and festive affair, and, when Maria stood in the mahogany-colored pulpit, from which great orators have been preaching the gospel of social responsibility for the past 180 years, I wiped away tears of gladness.

She spoke softly and sometimes stumbled over her rehearsed text, but she was steady and looked stunning with her curly dark hair pulled back. She was barely tall enough to let the new blue-and-white striped sweater peek over the lectern. I felt especially touched by the probing quest of her ending, "I am still wondering, if God put me here, what was my purpose here?"

Rites of Passage Sunday

In the mellowness of the moment, we had forgotten the rocky road of getting here, including the exhausting shopping spree for her nifty outfit. How many tops had I held up, cajoling, "How about this one? I think this would look real cute on you," only to hear the refrain, "I hate it."

Shopping was an ordeal for both of us. I was usually appalled by outrageous price tags and overwhelmed by choices, while Maria felt discouraged when she saw her plump reflection in the three-part mirrors of the changing booth. By the time we had bought the boldly striped top and size-fourteen miniskirt, she slumped into the chair of Woody's shoe department while I knelt before her with offerings of various leather loafers. She couldn't care less, and, when we finally loaded the bags into our hatchback, we were both exhausted and barely talking.

I've always hated shopping, and, when Maria was little, we lived on hand-me-downs from friends with awesome supply lines, including cute outfits of Sonny and Cher's precious offspring. But with the terrible teens came demands for the latest designer labels, triggering warfare in department stores. I thought of solving the problem with a clothing allowance, and suggested that she shop on her own, perhaps in the company of a savvy friend. She'd return from those shopping sprees with wild underwear and pricey perfume but not a stitch to replace fraying jeans and threadbare sweaters. So, if I wanted her to look presentable, as on the rites of passage Sunday, I had to embrace my phobia and dance with it through malls.

Part of our difficulty was Maria's size. Over the past nine months she had put on too many pounds, also due to the fact that she had had to skip soccer, basketball, and cheerleading because of her knee injury. The arthroscopy had not been successful, and, after complaining a lot and limping along, she had a second knee operation with the orthopedic surgeon a Washington weekly had pronounced as tops. She spent Christmas sitting bandaged under the tree, and by January hadn't healed well enough to zoom down the ski slopes as usual. By Easter she deserved a break, and, when the Warners, our good friends and former neighbors, said that there was still plenty of snow in Switzerland, we flew to Geneva where Jack had a two-year contract with an international organization. Our friends knew where to borrow the equipment, and it took about an hour to find Maria's correct size, with Jack patiently lugging every pair of boots from the shelves. Nothing fit. The frantic search for the right size seemed to turn into a test of whether Jack—and all of us crowding around—really cared. We did, and in the end we walked away with skies and poles and robotic boots, ready for Mont Blanc, the highest peak in the Alps, just over the border in France.

On a brilliantly sunny weekend, we took the cable car to ascend some 6,000 feet, and, under Jack's careful guidance, Maria navigated the slopes, falling a few times but always getting up unharmed. During our two years in Austria, she had become an excellent skier, and, despite surgeries and extra weight, her skills remained very much intact. She grinned behind fashionable sunglasses that mirrored sugar-white slopes under a true blue sky. At lunch, she heaped her plate to the brim and dug in lustily, while leaner fellow skiers dropped their forks and stared aghast. Everyone thought it, but nobody dared tell her that she was way overweight.

Except Dr. Schweizer, our trusted pediatrician. "You've got to lose some thirty pounds, also to help your knee," said the good doctor. She then outlined a daily meal plan. For a few weeks, Maria counted calories, but fast food after school or on the way to a little new job at the Wheaton Mall compromised attempts at a sensible diet.

She was a V-shaped Latin beauty with broad shoulders and narrow hips, different from the hourglass figures parading in teen magazines. She hid her bulging body under oversize men's shirts, but secretly yearned to have the lean and trim body of best friend Heather, a budding dancer at Duke Ellington, the District's public high school for the arts. Their friendship had begun to suffer from separation as well as from Maria's poor self-image. But Ellen, Heather's mom, remained Maria's loyal friend.

Once, when Ellen visited, I encouraged Maria to model a new outfit of miniskirt and blouse.

"Why don't you tuck it in?" Ellen coaxed gently when Maria appeared with the big blouse hanging over the skirt. "Show off your waist, girlfriend," said Ellen with her arm wrapped around Maria's shoulders. "It's here," she pointed, "just over your belly button." Maria obliged for the moment but then retreated again into the blouse's billowing shape, trying to hide her body as best she could.

And then all hell broke loose when I discovered discarded wrappings of over-the-counter diet pills. I also found an envelope containing a $50 check (she had her own account by then), and an order for more pills that promised a twenty-pound weight loss within two weeks.

"That's no way to lose weight," I said pounding the kitchen table. "You'll gain it all back as soon as you stop taking those pills, and you'll ruin your health in the process." How about Weight Watchers, I offered, a sensible diet program with group support. I had once joined the program after gaining five extra pounds from too much pastry during a holiday in Germany.

She'd never join a group, she said, rejecting my attempts at dialogue by slamming the door. But after three days of warfare, she gave in. On Tuesdays I now left work early to drive across Rock Creek Park to a Bethesda temple, where Maria was the only kid in a group of suburban matrons. She lost seven pounds that first week and was duly applauded as the top achiever. By the end of the summer she had lost twenty pounds.

I was baking french fries with just a few drops of oil and fixing turkey breast in a sauce of minus calories when the Warners rang the doorbell, back from Geneva. They had to stay for supper, I insisted. We'd stretch the meal with a big salad. Maria had joined Weight Watchers, I said by way of explaining our meager offerings.

"That's it!" Maria hissed. "How dare you tell everybody about my new diet!" She grabbed her backpack and stormed out of the house, leaving us dumbfounded around the table. The Warners were going to stay with us that summer while negotiating the purchase of a house just three blocks up the street. I had looked forward to our friendly togetherness, and Maria would also love their company, I assumed. But instead, the next weeks turned into a nightmare. My diary records the anguish: "It's been horrible—the worst phase of my parenting yet. Still have the scars on my arm from her attack after the day with Heather and Ellen."

It had been beastly hot, and the four of us had spent the Saturday at the idyllic Rock Creek Pool, where we had a membership. Returning home, Heather and Maria took over the bathroom, showering, washing their hair, coifing, primping, preening. I had to pee, I said, knocking on the door. Sorry, said Maria. I finally barged in, uninvited. After our friends had left, Maria unleashed her fury in a verbal attack and then, for added emphasis, grabbed the jar of powdered pink lemonade mix from the kitchen shelf and emptied it over my head. For a second I stood frozen like Lot's wife, staring at Maria who laughed at my glistening pink sight. Then rage swept through me and I grabbed her screaming. But, in the ensuing struggle, she was stronger. Her sharp fingernails dug into my flesh and scraped my upper arms, drawing blood. Seeing red, I let go. Crying, sticky, and bleeding I drove to Judy's home, just a few blocks away. I sobbed on her porch for an hour, while she listened, and sponged, cleaned, and bandaged my wounds. Judy, the single mom of two challenging children, always managed to stay calm, thanks also to a hefty dose of Prozac. Soothed by her kindness, I resolved that I was the adult and the mother, and therefore had to go home. On the drive back, I wondered whether Maria had meanwhile cleaned up the sticky mess around the kitchen sink. She hadn't and was holed up in her room with the TV blaring.

A week later, a friend sat at our garden table and pointed at my scars with some alarm, "What happened to you?" "Oh, just weeding some brambles," I mumbled, feeling Maria's piercing eyes on me. Now I knew why abused wives cover up. I felt shame over my failure to have a caring relationship with my daughter. And, except for Judy, I told no one.

With summer school over, Maria had a lot of time on her hands. She would sleep all morning and then itch to join the action of the night. I paid her to do projects around the house, but, with her chronic aversion toward instruction and direction, especially from her mom, her messy painting and weeding jobs left more cleanup than if I had done them myself.

For a few days, Barbara from Virginia came to visit. She was a year younger than Maria, and the girls had been playmates since Maria's arrival from Colombia. Now they were old enough to negotiate the subway and visit museums on the Mall. Since a group of colleagues and I were going to visit the recently opened Holocaust Museum, I invited the girls to come along. Maria was a favorite around the office, well known up and down the halls ever since she had been a toddler and had to tag along on snow days and other catastrophic occasions.

The Holocaust Museum was fast becoming the most visited site in DC. Laura, a Jewish colleague, had said that she didn't think she could set foot in the place, whereupon our enlightened boss decided that we should all join Laura on the pilgrimage. I remember passing through the museum's displays in a daze, with a lump in my throat. The exhibit started harmlessly enough with a Jewish middle-class family's home somewhere in Germany. Slowly their lives unraveled under the onslaught of Nazi persecution. I wept before the towering mountain of shoes in all sizes, remnants of incinerated lives.

Maria and Barbara stuck together and were watching film clips of medical experiments in concentration camps when I waved good-bye. Back home that evening, Maria was especially agitated and left the house in a huff when the food I served didn't please her. "She will be back," Barbara consoled me. Maria had mentioned friends in Mt. Pleasant, a Hispanic neighborhood, but Barbara didn't know where they lived.

"Don't worry, she'll be back," Barbara repeated. She was curled up on the bunk bed with a good book. I lingered in the doorframe, in need of the fourteen-year-old's counsel.

"It's not easy, you know, to go to the Holocaust Museum and realize that your mother is German," explained Barbara, whose father was Jewish and whose mother was a German immigrant, like me.

So I had another strike against me.

"Maria has the most severe case of hating me and the house and her life," I wrote in my diary. "It's so unsettling and scary, and renders me completely helpless."

At the beginning of the summer, I had asked Maria's counselor for a joint session. Halfway through, Maria had walked out. "She is transferring the feelings she has for her birth mother onto you," the wise Pat McArthur explained. At some level I understood. But how was I to live with this child, who raged against the woman who had abandoned her and, absent that woman, used me for a punching bag? "Whenever I bring up her birth mother, Maria says that there's nothing to talk about. But I know better," confided Pat.

With Pat off for the summer, we struggled on without much help. One night, Maria went to a movie and agreed that I should pick her up at ten. I waited at the exit until the last person had straggled out, and then realized that she had fooled me once again. Back home, I waited by the phone and then got into my car at midnight, driving around Silver Spring and the metro stop, until the last train had come and gone. I went back home.

I couldn't sleep and sat at the kitchen table until she came home around 1:30 in the morning.

"I saw you three times," she boasted. "Had to change my position so you wouldn't see me. I can't live with you and in this house. Forget it," she hissed, halfway up the stairs, looking down. "It's over, get over it," she shouted, as if ours was a casual affair.

"I can't," I said miserably.

"You're a joke. Your rules are laughable. I can't sleep with you in this house. I can only sleep with the people in Mt. Pleasant, there are six in that house." She wouldn't tell me who they were, of course.

"You've got to get tough," said my friend Marian.

"You've got to live your life as normally as you can," advised Ellen.

Heeding their advice, I told Maria once again that she was grounded and went to the Kennedy Center to see *Miss Saigon*, the new smash hit about love in wartime. At the show's dramatic climax, a full-size army helicopter with whirling blades descended onto the stage to whisk away a lucky few. *Where is the* deus ex machina *that will rescue me?* I wondered.

During intermission, I called Miss Maria and found her home and very cheerful. Upon my return, she reported the murder of the Colombian soccer player who had fouled a precious goal during that World Cup game we had watched. "Dreadful," we said and commiserated. As I prepared for bed, she took a shower and brushed her teeth. She was waiting for a phone call, she said.

Was she planning to go out?

No.

Was she expecting someone?

No.

She was just going to sit on the porch for a while, getting some fresh air, she said. As I moved around nervously, she came to assure me that she'd be in bed "in five minutes."

"Go to sleep," she said and closed my door. Wide awake, I listened to her every move. When all was quiet, I came out to check. She was gone. A car must have come to pick her up.

"I feel absolutely horrible," I wrote into my diary. "I don't know what to do." In the dark of the night, the fear of losing her—of already having lost her—dribbled through my veins with paralyzing force.

This wasn't the fear I had felt that day when two black kids held me up at gunpoint and drove away with my VW. It wasn't the fear I had felt when a burglar, half naked, stood by my bed in the middle of the night. "Get out," I had screamed at the top of my lungs, making him flee the house.

This was the fear of helplessness and hopelessness and of feeling trapped. Like the time I sat in a Berlin basement with bombs falling all around during the waning days of World War II, when I was seven, a refugee, and separated from my family.

My father had arranged for me to stay with Tante Benthlin, an older parishioner who had found refuge with relatives in a suburb. I'd be safer there, my father reasoned, while he stayed in the city at a Methodist hospital. My mother and three sisters were still stranded near the Russian front.

That night in Berlin, bombs exploded relentlessly, signaling the end. "Pray, child, pray," admonished Tante Benthlin. "Are the Russians coming?" I asked. "Yes," she whimpered. That's when I started shaking like a leaf. The Russians, I knew from whispered conversations, did unspeakable things to women, "… and even to children like her," an informant had said, pointing at me. Now the Russians were going to descend the cellar's stone steps, and I was trapped.

"Are they really coming right now?" I asked again.

"No, not tonight," clarified Tante Benthlin. Oh well, I thought, relaxing with a sigh. I could deal with bombs, was used to their attacks night after night, had lived with air raids most of my life. I knew I'd survive tonight.

Whenever Maria ran off, I felt trapped again in primal fear. Afraid of losing my mind, I kept scribbling in my diary. By two in the morning, I sometimes called my sister Beate, who had just finished breakfast in the Black Forest.

My sister was a good listener, but also gave advice. "You must put her into a boarding school," she said firmly. "There must be some pot of public funding for that child. And if you can't find it in the States, tell her that you'll put her into a Colombian boarding school. That may wake her up. You can't let her drive you crazy."

I bathed in Beate's passionate concern, but got defensive when she mentioned Maria's "… different set of genes, and what can you expect?"

As a graduate of the optimistic sixties, I believed that genetic handicaps and early traumas could heal in a loving and nurturing environment. I was convinced that I could provide such an environment. Part of my anguish was the realization that Maria might be beyond my fix-it zeal.

In August, my rescuing helicopter arrived in the shape of Apple Farm, a rural New Jersey arts and music camp that a musician friend had recommended. After seeing an inspiring video about 200 campers singing, dancing, performing, creating, and living their dreams, Maria decided that she might actually like harvesting vegetables and jazzing in a band. As soon as I had dropped her off at the chicken coop that had been converted into a primitive dorm, I drove off, singing Beethoven's *Freude, schöner Götterfunken* [Ode to Joy]" all the way home.

While Maria fell in love with the tenor saxophone, organized soccer games, and "adjusted very well to camp life," according to messages from her jolly Australian counselors, I breathed easy and took a week to visit my sister Claudia on Vancouver Island. I swam in the icy waters of Nanoose Bay, learned to shuck oysters and trap crabs, and I even borrowed a hat for high tea at the Empress Hotel in Victoria (where Barbara Streisand was denied admission for showing up in shorts).

To and from the island, I stopped in Seattle, my favorite city. Walking among the fishmongers and flower vendors in Pike Place Market, I renewed my vow to move here upon retirement. "Just three more years," I mumbled, smiling at absolutely everyone, including peddlers, junkies, and drunkards who were dozing in the doorways.

Back home on Alaska Avenue, I started inching my way through the debris in Maria's room every evening after work. After about ten days, I was finally able to see and scrub the floor and cart away moldy containers with cultures ripe for biological warfare. Once the room was tidy and clean, I bought a carpet in Maria's favorite blue, hung matching blinds on the three windows, put a denim bean bag into a reading nook, and painted the desk chair a royal blue. *What a lovely room*, I marveled, as I sprawled over the blue-and-white checkered quilt on her bed. *Will she appreciate my version of beauty and order?* I wondered.

I remembered my mother surprising me with a new look for my room after I returned from a summer in England at the age of seventeen. She had painted the hospital-white wardrobe and desk a pink-beige, and had sewn curtains, a bedspread, and matching pillow covers from cotton remnants. My mother thrived on ingenuity and remnants, and could make something stunning out of next to nothing, be it meals, clothing, or the home she pieced together after we had lost everything to war.

When I was a teen, my mother and I had our share of quarrels. She didn't approve of my best friend who got me to sneak cigarettes, didn't care for my way-out fashion statements, and got frustrated when she needed vinegar for the salad, for example, and discovered it by my messy sink because I had needed some to rinse my hair for a brilliant shine. She once kept a diary of her frustrations, and, when she read her litanies to me at the end of the day, I laughed out loud, especially over her search for the missing vinegar. Reluctantly, she laughed along. In a pinch, through church bazaars, houseguests, or her many illnesses, she could always count on me. And I knew that she loved me when I saw my gloriously transformed beige-pink and rose-colored room upon returning from England. I hugged and kissed her, something we didn't indulge in too often in those years.

Maria was into tearful farewells and bear hugs with campers, counselors, and favorite teachers when I arrived at Apple Farm to pick her up. "I've never cried so much in all my life," she sighed, settling in next to me. On the five-hour drive home, she talked about camp life with wonder and affection, vowing to return next year. She felt proud of her saxophone solo at the concert, really liked the cool guys in her photography course, and had received kudos for organizing popular soccer games. Back home, I perked my ears when she climbed the stairs to her new blue room. There was a pause, followed by a casual, "I like it." She dumped the contents of her trunk onto the new carpet, her way of making the place her own.

Her mellow mood didn't last a week, and soon anger burst forth like a bear after hibernation. "You thought that four weeks of camp would make a difference. Well, it didn't. I still hate you and this house, and I can't live here. You'd better figure something out or I'll be out there again," she threatened ominously.

I should either arrange for boarding school, or I should get her foster parents, she demanded. A good neighbor had offered earlier to take Maria in for a while, but then her eighteen-year-old returned from Europe and needed the room. I couldn't wait for school and counseling to start.

Gene Chapin, a psychologist at Chelsea School, had agreed to take us on with Pat McArthur assisting as Maria's coach. Our first session at the end of August started badly. Maria said that she was tired, and put her head on the table. No, she didn't know why we were meeting and couldn't care less. "Okay," said Chapin, known for his magic push and pull. He handed each of us a piece of paper. "Now both of you put down five things you want and five things you need." I started scribbling, while Maria stared at her blank page. Once I had read "celebrations" among my wants and "health and enough money" among my needs, she perked up, apparently relieved that my lists didn't mention her behavior.

With newfound alacrity, she soon scribbled down her list of needs and wants, including late-night outings and a bigger allowance. During ensuing negotiations, Pat and Maria would huddle next door to figure out responses to my offers of incentives. As our sessions continued, they became lighthearted with occasional bursts of laughter over Maria's outrageous demands or counteroffers. She thrived on hairsplitting arguments, and, when she hinted that she'd like to become a lawyer, Pat cried, "Heaven help us," and we all agreed.

We were almost looking forward to our Wednesday sessions and discussions of needs and wants. Mine soon included a biking trip along the Danube with my sister Claudia. She and I had been fantasizing about the ten-day sojourn for some time, and, with newly established peace at our home, Claudia urged that we plan the outing for October. We discussed my trip over the course of several Wednesday sessions. "Why not?" said Chapin. "This will be your opportunity to shine, Maria," he admonished, and she nodded seriously. The separation will do us good, I reasoned, wiping away cobwebs of doubt from the crevices of my brain.

Providing for Maria was the top priority during my preparations. Who would look out for her? Our wonderful downstairs neighbor Mary had been transferred to Colorado Springs, and I had just finished renovating the apartment when a neighbor inquired about the space for a journalism intern who came highly recommended. Thus we met Sonya and Michael, a newly married interracial couple. We liked them instantly and they, in turn, liked my offer of free rent in exchange for keeping track of Maria while I was gone. The three would share evening meals for which I provided funds, and they grinned at the prospect of joking around the kitchen table. They seemed to have a lot in common. Michael, who taught math and chess, was sports obsessed, just like Maria. On the two weekends of my absence, Jack and Jane Warner, who lived down the street, Ellen, and Maria's favorites, Sam and Nancy, promised outings, movies, fun, and games. I gave Jack Warner power of attorney.

Claudia and I met in Frankfurt and had barely hugged our sisters in the Black Forest when the first phone calls came in. Jack reported that he had gone to our house on Friday night to pick up Maria for the weekend but she hadn't answered. Letting himself in with a key, he went from room to room, searching for clues. He contacted the police and reported her missing. When he returned the next morning, he heard a rumble in the attic, followed by Maria, her bosom buddy Johna (who was also adopted), and an unknown boy, marching down the stairs. They had apparently spent the night in the attic, leaving candle stumps, Frito bags, and blankets in their wake. "We've been looking for you all over and have been worried sick," Jack told them. They ignored him, as if he were a ghost, and vanished around the block. Jack and Johna's dad spent the rest of that Saturday looking for the girls at all the nearby malls. "I was supposed to have lunch with Nelson Mandela," said Johna's father, a chaplain at Howard University. "Instead I'm searching for my missing child."

The two men looked in vain, but late that night the Warners received a call from the police. Maria and Johna had been caught shoplifting baseball mitts in a sporting goods store. Jack found a suit and tie in the back of his closet and looked his most respectable when he went to the police station to retrieve a defiant Maria.

"Let's sit down and talk," said Jane, who had felt frantic over the past two days.

"There's nothing to talk about. I'm going home."

"No, you're staying and we're going to talk."

"You can't make me."

"I'll lock the door," Jane threatened.

"Then I'll escape through the window."

They were both screaming by then, and someone called the police. The officer who arrived supported Maria's wish to be in her own home. With Sonya and Michael downstairs, the request seemed reasonable to him, and the battle-weary Warners acquiesced. Past midnight, the cruiser delivered Maria to our doorstep.

"Should I come home?" I asked Jack, after listening to this alarming news. "Well, Jane thinks you should. But I think Maria has stabilized. I think you can go ahead," said Jack, the father of four children.

I talked to Maria. I didn't really know what to say and handed the receiver to Claudia, who found a soothing tone. They had become best buddies over the years. My athletic and competitive sister knew a tomboy when she saw one, and had lots of fun egging Maria on, be it on a hiking scramble along the Potomac, or teaching her to swim during a vacation in Mexico's Yucatan.

When I was little, my six-years-older sister tried hard to shape me into her daring and strong partner. She failed, because I was a hopeless wimp who started crying when ghost stories got too scary and tobogganing slopes too steep. Thoroughly disgusted, Claudia often dropped me off at home after January outings, and then returned to deadly slides and zero temperatures. In my daughter, Claudia had found her match and always arrived with the neatest presents, like the teal green pantsuit and matching roller skates that came with introductory lessons.

Now I listened intently as the two discussed recent events. "Don't worry about me," Maria assured my sister, "I'm okay."

"Let's go," said Claudia.

I remember our biking trip through a wall of October fog. We started in a charming Baroque village in Germany, veiled by morning mists, and arrived a week and 260 miles later in Vienna, wrapped in fog. In between, we passed celebrated vineyards, ruins of ancient fortresses, and famous medieval monasteries. It was late in the season, and most tourists were back home. Sometimes we didn't meet a soul all day; we always ended at dusk in some small village and cozy inn. We soaked our increasingly sore seats in bubble baths, ate caloric meals that ended with creamy desserts, and then sank into starched sheets and fluffy featherbeds. This was before ubiquitous cell phones, so no emergencies interrupted our bliss.

In Klosterneuburg, a suburb of Vienna, we paused at the beautiful Gothic cathedral and remembered that our father had been born in this town. Once, on a family outing, he told us the story of revisiting his first home. He was already well established in his ministry and the father of four daughters when he rang the bell at his birth house and was met by a woman in an apron, a housekeeper. She welcomed him into the living room, where an old blind man sat at a house organ. "Sure," said the old man, "have a look around."

Returning to the living room after his tour, my father asked his host to play something for him. The old man obliged with a prelude by Anton Bruckner, who once had been organist at Klosterneuburg's cathedral. After the last chord, my father offered to reciprocate and began reciting the Twenty-third Psalm: "The Lord is my shepherd; I shall not want … Goodness and mercy shall follow me all the days of my life …"

They sat in silence for a while. "You're a professional," the old man then said. "So are you," bowed my father.

We, however, were no professional bikers, as our very sore bottoms let us know. When we stopped to watch a train zooming by on its way to the inner city, I pleaded that we board one for the last few miles. I was so sore I could hardly walk. "No way," Claudia said firmly. "We've made it this far, we can pedal the last few miles." Our childhood patterns still prevailed, I noticed, as I followed her lead lamely.

"Call Jack," was the message, awaiting me in Vienna. "The consensus is that you should come home as soon as possible," said Jack when I reached him. Maria's school attendance had been sporadic, and she had invited unknown characters—a girl named Rosie and a young man, Kameo—to live with her in our house. Downstairs, Sonya and Michael had checked them out and had at first thought that the *ménage à trois* might work, but subsequently requested that Rosie and Kameo leave. Maria was pissed and drove off with Kameo in my car, returning every day to fetch some clothing. Attempting triage, Maria's counselor Pat asked Jack and Michael to join the Wednesday session, hoping that the two good-looking and friendly men could coax Maria back into the straight and narrow. But she remained obstinate and withdrawn, and, seeing her spiraling down, Pat offered Maria a choice: stay at home or get locked up in protective custody. Maria chose home alone, with Sonya and Michael keeping their vigil.

On the following weekend, Sam and Nancy picked her up for a ballgame, dinner, and a movie. She stayed overnight at their Connecticut Avenue apartment, and on Monday morning Sam dropped her off at school on his way to the University of Maryland. But for the past two days, Jack reported, Maria hadn't been at school.

I felt stunned by Jack's account and took the night train back to the Black Forest, picked up my suitcase, paid the penalty for returning early, and boarded the next flight to DC. My seat mate was a retired German ship captain who was headed to his second home in Costa Rica. We told each other tales of our lives, and, just before landing, I unburdened my motherly woes. "What do I do and say when I get home?" I wondered out loud.

"Well, first you give her a big hug," he advised. Of course, I nodded. The drudgery of mothering had almost made me forget that I loved Maria dearly. When I put the key into our front door, the alarm system announced my arrival loudly. I found Maria in bed. "I'm not feeling well," she said, stiffly tolerating my embrace. She didn't care to talk about her escapades. Neither did Sonya or Michael when I knocked downstairs.

"You didn't tell me that taking care of your daughter is a twenty-four-hour job," hissed Sonya. The couple's deposit check, I discovered, had bounced, and anger camouflaged their embarrassment over lack of funds. I cut my losses, found some food, and prepared a meal.

The next morning, I drove Maria to school and briefly stopped by Pat McArthur's office. "Thank God, you're back," she said. "You're the only person who can keep this child together." I wondered how, as I began to stalk Maria like a scorned lover. We were both subdued and apprehensive, waiting for a spark from somewhere that could blow us all to smithereens.

While she was at school, I sorted through the pile of clothing on her bedroom floor, some still with price tags, making me wonder whether the Nike sweat suit and brand-new parka were bounty from a shoplifting spree. I sorted the clothes into his and her piles, and when Kameo next called, I told him that he could pick up his stuff in a plastic bag next to the garbage can in the back alley. "You are putting my clothes next to the garbage?" he asked indignantly. "Yes. And if you ever show your face at my doorstep, I'll have you arrested for messing with a minor," I told him. The line went dead.

Next, I found a reference to Rosie's suburban school and called the counselor, who seemed to know the girl well. Yes, she would tell Rosie to call. When she did, I asked that she come with her parents that evening to retrieve her size thirty-eight bras, miniskirts, and pregnancy testing kit. When she and her parents ascended our long garden steps that night, I knew at a glance that we were all in the same adoption boat.

Rosie, I learned, was a year older than Maria, a bright biracial kid with a long list of transgressions, including leaving her keys in someone's car, resulting in the burglary of her parents' house. Rosie's parents suggested wearily that I change all my locks, especially since several of our house keys were missing.

On Saturday, after the locksmith had left, I drove Maria across town to a soccer field for goalie training. In the evening, I was to meet Marian for a concert at the Kennedy Center, but I cancelled when Maria said that she wanted to see a movie. "All right, let's go!"

She liked to sit up front and I in back, and so we found our seats with a see-you-later wave. After the girl-gets-boy ending of the raunchy juvenile flick, I waited at the exit with a sinking feeling. She wasn't in the crowd, and, when I returned to my car, I found a note under the windshield "Can't stay at home, have to think. Will be back soon." I drove home and reported her to the police as missing. When she came home the next morning at nine, I called the police again and two officers with clanking gear—one black officer, one white, DC's politically correct combination—bent over Maria who was crouching in the corner of the staircase like a caught kitten.

"Hey, I think I've seen you around," lied the first officer. "You've got a nice home and a nice mom," intoned the second. "You'll get into real trouble if you keep running away. And some day you may not be able to come home again," they warned as they left.

"The only thing stupider than the police is you," spat Maria, as she went to bed. Meanwhile, I received phone calls from hostile males. "So you're Maria's mother," said one know-it-all. "You seem to have an accent. Is it German? You are probably racist." Maria, listening in, snickered in the background. I felt deeply betrayed. Maria's hostility was escalating, making me wonder if I was safe within my own four walls. I changed the access code to her voice mail, and, when she realized that she could no longer retrieve her messages, she threatened that she'd soon leave for good. "Nobody, not even the police, will ever find me," she warned. I noticed that her passport was missing from the drawer in my desk.

After huddling with the two therapists at Chelsea, we scheduled a family session for the following Wednesday. Maria came in late and refused to sit down. Standing by the door, she informed us that she was finished with counseling, once and for all.

"Maria," warned Chapin, "if you leave this room, it will have grave consequences."

"I don't care," she said, slamming the door.

"Have her arrested," Chapin advised, turning to me. "The situation calls for drastic intervention. She is a person in need of supervision. Call the police and start the process."

I was stunned. Had we really arrived at this point of no return? Could I ask the police to arrest my child and commit her into the quagmire of DC's juvenile justice system? Pat led me into the teacher's lounge where I made my first phone call, and then broke down, shaking. "I can't do this," I said sobbing. "You have to, for Maria's sake," she countered softly.

I kept dialing numbers and got the feeling that our middle-class drama was a low priority in crime-ridden DC. Walking the hallways of the downtown courthouse, I finally found a pompous schmuck who enjoyed displaying his prosecutorial powers. "Give me the facts," he demanded, and then called Pat, who confirmed that Maria had threatened to leave home, mother, and country this very Friday. He called Detective Washington, who lumbered into the office with obvious disdain for his boss. "Interview the kid," the prosecutor barked.

That evening, Maria acted subdued, and, when the doorbell rang at nine, I wondered if I might end up in handcuffs for crying wolf. But sitting between us in the rocking chair, Maria's hostile attitude quickly returned without much prodding.

"Maria, you are lucky to have a very nice home," said Detective Washington, surveying the antiques and modern art in our living room. "And you have a mother who cares about you."

"This is not my mother, and this is not my home," growled Maria.

"This is not your mother, and you don't want to stay here?"

"No."

He paused.

"Let me ask you again: Do you want to stay in this home with your mother?"

"No."

"You leave me no choice but to take you away. Get your coat, take off your belt and shoelaces."

While he scribbled into his notebook, she did as told. Anger flashed through her deliberately slow motions. "You'd better straighten your attitude," said Washington who sensed the static, "or I'll take you away in handcuffs."

They left, and I remained in my chair, as if paralyzed. A minute later, Washington was back, looking for something he thought he had left behind. *By now, she is probably handcuffed and shackled*, I thought. *He wouldn't leave this kid unfettered in a cruiser.*

When I saw her again two days later, she looked bedraggled and unkempt, shuffling into the courtroom in her high-tops without laces. She had spent the first night locked up in the courthouse, and the second in a women's facility where she had shared the cell with a sixteen-year-old prostitute who had a one-year-old child. "That girl has a horrible life," Maria had told her court-appointed lawyer, an elegantly dressed middle-aged woman whom I had just met outside the courtroom.

"You have no idea how many girls would envy you for your good life," the lawyer had told Maria. "Maybe she'll now come to her senses," the lawyer said to me wistfully. Our court-ordered relationship had started rather rocky. She was to represent Maria's best interests and treated me like an ogre for putting this child behind bars. "Maria moves awkwardly," the lawyer observed. "Put her in a charm school, get her some dance lessons," she advised, spinning around on her high heels. *Give me a break*, I thought.

I had been asked to bring clothes and toiletries, and I plunked down the big black travel bag next to the lawyer. I had also brought an envelope with photos of our dog, Magic, our house, Maria bending over a drawing at school, and Maria in the pulpit of All Souls during the rites of passage ceremony, just six months earlier. I had enclosed a copy of her essay, "Do I believe in God?"

The lawyer grabbed the documents and took them over to where Maria stood. They huddled, and then the lawyer approached the bench and handed the photos and essay to a white-haired, grandfatherly judge.

He spread the contents of the envelope before him and started reading.

"To believe in God is to believe that all our stars are lucky ones," Maria had written.

He stopped and peered over the rim of his glasses. Before him stood a despairing mother and a disheveled child, looking almost Godforsaken.

11.

THE BUDDING ARTIST

The grandfatherly judge decided to place Maria into Tower House, a shelter run by the YWCA. It was located in Anacostia, the District's poorest African-American neighborhood.

Tower House was an inconspicuous, two-story home in a residential section. Like other houses, it had iron bars on windows, but its front door stayed unlocked, giving the eight resident girls the choice to come and go according to house rules, or run away and get locked up for good.

Before her transfer to Tower House, Maria had stayed for three days in a juvenile detention center. She never talked about that experience, but it must have been scary.

"She's lucky that she got away," one of the matrons at Tower House informed me. "The detention center has a reputation—inmates often gang up on newcomers. The girls have access to a Coke machine and use the tops of the cans like razors to attack girls in the shower—especially light-skinned girls like Maria. I've seen a few arrive here all scarred."

I shuddered as I plunked down Maria's schoolbag and clothing. I had felt jittery on my first drive through unfamiliar Anacostia, where the police kept a low profile, and I seemed to be the only white face for miles around. I worried about Maria's safety, worried whether I had made the right decision to have her arrested, worried whether I'd ever get her home again.

"Maria is exactly where she ought to be," our friend Ellen assured me after visiting Maria at the shelter. I had hoped that Ellen, a Presbyterian minister among her many avocations, could break through Maria's hostility and confusion. She had always had great rapport with Maria. Sitting with her

117

on the bunk of the shelter's upstairs dormitory, Ellen tried her best to coax my child from behind a stone wall.

"Maria says that she has finally found her true home," Ellen reported. "She says she never wants to return to Alaska Avenue. She didn't want to talk, and we sat together for a while in silence, and then I left her. I talked to her caretakers, and it turns out that one of them went to school with my sister. I told them to take good care of Maria—that she is a very special child to many of us."

I cried, especially when Ellen added ominously, "I'm afraid that now that Maria is in the system, she'll have a hard time getting out." But I also felt comforted by Ellen's report, and, as I got to know the shelter's staff, I came to admire the women's commitment to the girls in their care. All had been placed there because they were out of control and in need of supervision. They weren't inclined toward forming a loving sorority. Their razor-sharp interactions had been honed during early combats of survival, and Maria, not familiar with their style, learned to keep out of the fracas.

Part of her escape was Chelsea, her school way up north beyond the District's border. In order to get there via public transportation, Maria had to get up an hour earlier than usual and make two transfers on the subway. With her lousy sense of direction, I worried that she might get lost. But there she was, moving up the escalator from the green to the red line at Gallery Place, where I also transferred on my way to work.

I stopped in my tracks when I spotted her, an adolescent girl with a bouncing pigtail, still dripping from her morning shower. She looked pale, and her face was drawn tight. Before I could move, she had disappeared like an apparition into the throng of commuters.

Despite the many institutional transfers after her arrest, she had missed only four days of school, and Chelsea soon turned into her home away from home. She had good relationships with her teachers and was glad to sit again next to Johna, her accomplice in previous escapades. After Maria had been arrested, Johna also threatened to run away from home forever. She threw such a furious and violent tantrum that the police advised her parents to place her in a shelter.

At school, the girls became inseparable. They exchanged survival tactics of shelter life, railed against their stupid parents, and, after a few weeks, confessed to each other pangs of homesickness and twitches of affection for parents, who looked better with every passing day.

Besides the fact that they were both adopted, Maria and Johna shared a love for art. At the beginning of the school year, Pat Ginger, their multi-talented teacher, had offered a handful of very gifted students a double art class that met every day, resulting in unprecedented creativity. I've often observed that children with learning disabilities are remarkable artists, making me wonder whether their talent is a gift at birth or develops as a refuge from learning and emotional handicaps.

Maria displayed talent early on. At Barbara Chambers Children's Center, she had painted masterworks at three, applying color with powerful strokes at an easel that was about her height. A neighbor with a reputable art collection asked for one of Maria's pink-and-blue mirages for her bedroom wall.

When she was nine, Maria returned from summer camp at the Cathedral School with a little table sawed and nailed from wooden planks. The mother of a camper, who had shuttled several neighborhood children from camp, was amazed at Maria's solid piece of furniture. "Valerie," she let me know, "everybody else's project fell apart as we unloaded." I still have the table. It serves as nightstand in my bedroom.

In Vienna, Maria produced amazing sculptures and feisty drawings under the guidance of a talented artist at the American School. I remember one project in particular. The students were given copies of a medieval woodcut depicting a man in a landscape. The man's head was missing, and the students were encouraged to draw in its place emblems of themselves. One boy, Maria reported, drew his butt, ha-ha! She completed the man with a social-realism fist that seemed to belong on a Marxist poster. The fist's knuckles and tendons were straining for a punch. I showed the drawing to Maria's wimpy therapist, in case she didn't know what we were up against.

During her years in public schools, Maria's talent remained dormant. At Shepherd Elementary, she once received a prize for neatest and fastest seamstress in a quilting competition. But at Deal, she earned a C because she didn't copy her teacher's efforts properly. She wasn't interested and couldn't really see the drawing at the blackboard because she needed glasses, as it turned out.

Chelsea offered a welcome return to creativity. I had started framing her drawings and paintings when she was fourteen. A designer and retired former colleague, who ran a framing business from his basement, always presented Maria's art to best effect. He cleaned smudges on a pencil drawing, for example, because, being a lefty, her hand's movement sometimes smeared the paper. He cleverly floated a still life of a guitar and pumpkin so none of the important strings at the edge of the paper would be lost under the frame. Maria's works hung on our living room walls and seemed to fit right into our collection that included works of Alexander Calder, Leonard Baskin, and Bruce Carter.

I was an awed and passionate supporter of Maria's talent, especially since I had been stunted early in my artistic efforts. I still remember the hour of my miserable failing. It was in art class in fifth grade. We were into watercolors and were assigned to paint flowers in the market from memory and without guidance. Before I knew it, my rendition was awash in red, purple, yellow, and green with colors running all over the warped paper. Once more, what I had clearly envisioned turned into a catastrophe. Aghast and immobilized, I stared at the soggy mess as my teacher on her rounds stopped behind my desk. Without uttering a word she moved on. "She shook her head," my neighbor reported with a snicker. My efforts clearly were beyond redemption.

Instead of art, writing became my private refuge. I got my first diary, bound in green linen, on my eleventh birthday and have kept scribbling ever since, especially during times of agony and ecstasy. When Maria stayed out beyond agreed-upon times, I resorted to my diary. "I will write until she comes home. I will not move pen from paper until I hear the key in the front door," I wrote. Sometimes she rescued me from mindless lamentations; sometimes I slumped over in numbed exhaustion.

For Maria, creating art was a way of feeling whole, especially during times of chaos. While at Tower House, she worked on several big pieces. One was a seven-foot charcoal of Zeus, grimly descending from on high. The black image with blinding white highlights looked more like a menacing underworld monster than the god who reigned on Olympus. Zeus was way too scary to hang on a wall in our house, but a five-foot *papier-mâché* African mask ended up dominating our dining room. Maria worked on the mask for months, adding layer upon layer of newsprint from *The Washington Post*, soaking, gluing, shaping the skull with nostrils, eyes, and horns, and finally varnishing the piece in brown and black. The mask looked daunting. "Stunning … amazing," said a curator, who came at year's end to review the students' show.

The process of our reconciliation evolved parallel to Maria's unprecedented creativity. During the first few weeks at Tower House, when Maria insisted that she had finally found her true home and would never ever want to live with me again on Alaska Avenue, I sent her artsy postcards. The first, a Frida Kahlo self-portrait, carried a short message about our dog, "Magic misses you." Then a Diego Rivera image of a watermelon informed her, "The password on my office computer is Consuelo." I kept the messages short and signed them with, "Love, Mom." After a dozen of these postcards, the matron at the shelter called.

"Are you sending Maria these postcards?" she asked.

"Yes."

"But Maria says that the cards are from her birth mother!"

The matron also told me that a young man had called and asked to speak to Maria. He was her cousin, he had said. "Now, are you a cousin on her mother's or her father's side?" asked the matron, fishing for the young man's identity. The line went dead. I was afraid that Kameo, whose plastic bag of clothing still sat next to our garbage can, had tracked Maria down. I soon found out more about him than I cared to know.

In the aftermath of Maria's arrest, I faithfully attended weekly meetings of Tough Love, a parent support group. One Wednesday, upon arrival, I found the session had been cancelled. I stood with another mother before closed doors. We decided to counsel with each other and settled into the pew of a nearby church. "You go," the other mother said and let me delve into the saga of my errant child. I told her about Maria befriending Kameo, getting arrested for shoplifting, and then inviting the young man to stay at our home while I bicycled along the Danube. The woman nodded all along, as if she knew my story. When I mentioned the mountain of clothing the houseguests had left behind, she interrupted, "And in the heap was a white parka with a Disney World emblem. It belongs to my daughter!"

I learned that Kameo had an uncanny sense for identifying adopted girls, and had courted the woman's fifteen-year-old for weeks with roses. After he had been thrown out of the house, he was rediscovered living in the family's basement. They chased him out, and the daughter ran after him. They slept on bare floors of filling station restrooms until the girl was caught shoplifting. "He enticed her to do it and then grimaced into the store's camera, pointing at my daughter, calling attention to her stealing," the outraged mother reported.

The woman followed me home that night to retrieve her daughter's parka from the plastic bag that sat next to our garbage can. A couple of days later, the whole bag was gone. I felt enmeshed in a sinister network and wondered if we'd ever escape its grip unscathed.

At the time of Maria's arraignment, the court had ordered a battery of tests. I was convinced that Maria was out of her right mind, but the results proved me wrong. Her oppositional streak ran rampant, the psychologist told me, and her reading and writing skills were four years below grade level, despite a very high overall IQ. *What else is new?* I wondered.

Well, her change of mind was new. After Maria's initial euphoria over having escaped parental supervision, the shelter's strict house rules and the residents' knifing interactions soon made home on Alaska look cozy. During telephone conversations, Maria was polite and respectful and soon begged me to let her come home. I held out because I wanted that new attitude to mature.

The next time we appeared in court for a progress report, the Power House matron mentioned Kameo's frequent phone calls. Listening in on the conversations, she had been amazed that Maria listened to Kameo's threats and insults with the passivity of a lamb. The judge sternly advised Maria to sever the relationship, and, pale and trembling, she promised to comply.

"I stood where you're standing three times while growing up," the African-American judge told Maria. "If it hadn't been for my loving parents, I wouldn't be sitting here today. You are lucky to have a mother who deeply cares about you."

Based on a note I had slipped the judge earlier, he ordered Maria to participate in family counseling. My attempts to resume with Gene Chapin and Pat McArthur had faltered when Maria walked out of a scheduled session. She rightly suspected that the two counselors had helped to get her arrested. "Get a new and neutral therapist," Chapin advised, adding, "I'm afraid she'll end up locked in an institution."

The matrons at Tower House recommended Dr. Casey, who had been successful with other residents. A mountain of a woman, Dr. Casey held forth squeezed into a swivel chair. She recorded our grievances onto a yellow pad and once in a while asked for clarification, like: Why did I object to Maria and a friend climbing with the boom box onto the top of our roof? I had to explain at length the slant of the roof, accessible through Maria's bedroom window, the dangers of falling off, and the hazards of traffic slowing down, so drivers could take in the spectacle above. Dr. Casey finally got it and made a note. She kept professional advice to a minimum, making me wonder what I was paying for. Maria, however, let it all hang out and, feeling ever so much lighter, bounced out of the sessions toward the elevator, while I dragged behind. Dr. Casey was black, Maria was brown, and my white skin felt at a disadvantage.

After filling many pages on the legal pad, Dr. Casey suggested that we draw up a contract. It stipulated that Maria had to tidy her room only every other week before the cleaning team arrived with pail and broom. But the top paragraph of our contract said that I was entitled to know where and with whom she spent her free time. Maria balked.

"How would you feel if your mother left and didn't come home until the next day, Maria?" Dr. Casey coaxed.

"I wouldn't care," she shrugged. "My birth mother left me."

"Maria, I will never leave you," I countered.

Pause.

And again, "Maria I will never leave you."

Longer pause.

And then we returned to the nitty-gritty of our possible and probable coexistence.

Just before Thanksgiving, the shelter asked if Maria could spend the holiday in my care. Tower House would close so the caregivers could celebrate with their own families. Luckily, my friend Katie came through with an invitation to celebrate with her extended family. Katie's house on the Chesapeake Bay always offered holiday festivities fit for a Hallmark commercial, and this Thanksgiving followed established traditions. While the turkey roasted in the oven, we took a walk to the windy tip of the peninsula; we made cider from the farm's last windfalls, taking turns grinding apples through the old-fashioned press. In the late afternoon, we stuffed ourselves with turkey, all the trimmings, and an assortment of pies. And, in the evening, we passed the guitar around the circle for songs before a fire. A photo shows Maria stretched out at my feet while I lead with my favorite, "Bring Me a Rose in Wintertime." Maria isn't singing along, but looks content and comfy.

Four weeks later, we were back at Katie's cove for Christmas. The house was ablaze with lights, and even the dog and cats sported red bows. There were three decorated trees, including one at the end of the dock, reflecting sparkles onto the black waters at night. A mountain of presents under the tree included silly and modest gifts, like the package of white rice and a separate package of bouillon cubes for Katie's partner, the master of few recipes. By midday we had finally opened the last package and sat buried in wrappings and ribbons.

"Okay, let's start cooking," Katie proclaimed, stretching with a satisfied yawn.

"Why don't we first tidy up a bit?" I suggested.

"Oh no," said Katie who is German, "that would be too German."

"I'm glad you said that," Maria quipped. "If I had said that, I'd be back in jail."

We had a good laugh, and I promised to ignore the mess.

At the end of January, Maria spent her sixteenth birthday at the shelter. On my way to work, I dropped off a basket at the house of a classmate who would bring it to Maria at school. On top of the basket, filled with Maria's favorite cranberry cookies, sat a teddy bear wearing a big red bow and wishing her a happy day.

The basket was a big hit. Maria distributed cookies throughout the day and embraced the latest addition to her stuffed animal collection. The birthday teddy reappeared a few weeks later in an acrylic painting, surrounded by a sun, moon, and stars. Its cuddly cuteness and round proportions express endearment, and the celestial bodies in the background project a heartfelt longing toward the whole universe. The cheerful teddy and the sinister Zeus made an odd couple on the roller coaster of this budding artist's troubled soul. They were light and dark, yin and yang, Maria's favorite symbol. Years later, she incorporated yin and yang into a drawing of two colorful birds feeding on a swing.

Maria left the shelter in February, in time for my birthday. I was touched that she got our two resident radiologists to help her sing "Happy Birthday." She beamed when she presented a homemade card and Hershey kisses. Those first weeks back home felt like a honeymoon.

I'm not sure who mentioned a boarding school first, but at Easter we were flying to New Mexico to visit a school near Santa Fe. On the weekend in Albuquerque, we took in a Native American festival. We watched entire villages perform dances, ate flatbread fresh from the adobe ovens, and watched jewelry in the making. Maria was especially fascinated by the dancing, which was accompanied by drums, shouting, and chanting. She sat at the edge of the circle and drew busily onto her sketch pad. As she looked around, she saw girls with dark, thick hair and broad shoulders who could have been relatives. She was clearly among her ancestral tribe. But she wasn't as heavy and broad as most, and, with her glasses, pen and paper, she looked like the sister who had gotten away.

Back at school, she poured festival images onto her canvas. Her triptych, *The Vanishing Native American Culture,* depicted tepees, a dancer moving away from the viewer, and the head of an Indian chief. She worked especially hard to achieve the transparency of the old Indian's face. "Look, Mom, I finally got it," she said as she nudged me in the middle of the night, crouching by my bed with the finished painting. It showed the chief's face dissolving into a starry night.

By year's end, Maria had assembled an impressive portfolio of paintings, drawings, and sculptures, in addition to a thick book on art history that documented examples from antiquity to the present time. Pat Ginger awarded Maria with Chelsea's Certificate of Achievement in Art at a school assembly. As part of the ceremony, Pat and Maria staged a dialogue on the Mexican muralist Diego Rivera.

"What was his full name?" Pat prompted.

"Diego Maria de la Concepción Juan Nepomuceno Estanislao de la Rivera y Barrientos Acosta y Rodríguez," Maria rattled off. She was smitten with the poetic length of the painter's name, and, while she could never match it, she signed her own ever-lengthening name—Maria Consuelo Kreutzer-Mendez—with gusto onto her own creations.

At sixteen, she bathed in artistic achievement, followed by exhibits at All Souls Unitarian Church and the downtown YWCA. She also started selling. Ellen bought the *Vanishing Indian Chief* and Maria wrote a dedication on the back of the painting:

To Ellen,

Thanks for all you have done for me. I wish you all the best in all you do.

I love you.

There are no stars like the one of memory.

God will always be there for you and me and even when it is hard to predict.

Sam and Nancy bought a painting of potted plants, and Peter Miller, Maria's math teacher, bought the teddy bear for his then-girlfriend.

The teddy bear became the symbol for the Maria Consuelo Fund at Chelsea, set up by family and friends to honor students who follow in Maria's artistic footsteps. At the memorial service, two of Maria's paintings flanked the pulpit.

"I am especially struck by this painting over here," said Janice Grand, pointing to the *Vanishing Indian Chief*. "Coming from Latin America, Maria was *mestizo;* she was a Latina, but she also shared roots in the indigenous culture, and we see part of that in this painting. I am an artist, and Maria and I shared our artwork at times," Janice, a co-leader at the memorial service, explained. "Art is a place where you give form to feeling, it is a place where things come together, and you learn things about yourself that you can't in any other way. And Maria found in her art a place to express a side too deep for words."

A tearful Pat Ginger remembered Maria as "one of my most talented students … perhaps the best I've ever had."

Surrounded by her art

12.

SOLEBURY

At the end of March, Solebury invited us to visit their boarding school in Pennsylvania, and so we drove north on Interstate 95, and then veered off to coast along the Delaware and the spot where General Washington had crossed the river in pursuit of the British.

It seemed that not much had changed in Bucks County over the past two hundred years. Fieldstone houses and Colonial-era picket fences lined the narrow, winding road that led over bridges just wide enough for the passage of a single car. Meadows of daffodils, iris, and tulips colored the landscape, and, by the time we arrived at the simple sign, "Solebury School, Founded 1925," we two foreign-born city slickers were bowled over by bucolic beauty and early Americana.

Solebury had been founded by a group of young teachers who were short on money and long on idealism. They bought an old farm, converted barns into classrooms, added dormitories, and began an informal, close-knit educational community where students, calling their teachers by first names, were encouraged to think creatively, develop individual talents, and prepare for citizenship in the wider world.

Exploring the sprawling campus, we walked through light-filled studios displaying exquisite art; the theatre, still housed in an original barn; the architectural gem of a gym; and a happy hole in the wall that served as student hangout and café.

When the bell signaled the end of the academic day, students headed for practice on the athletic fields—past ducks on a pond and over the wooden bridge that spanned a gurgling brook. Twenty percent of the 180 students were minorities.

One of the reasons we had applied was the school's center for learning-disabled students. Tom Ungar had started the learning skills program in 1985. Ten years later, by the time we applied, it had grown to include twenty-five students and was known as one of the best LD programs in the country.

Ungar, a kind and balding man, spent two and a half hours with Maria, testing her in reading, writing, science, and math. He also talked with her at length. Her math and science skills were good and at her tenth-grade level, he found. However, her reading of rows of unrelated words put her at fifth-grade level, and her reading of paragraphs, at sixth. He asked her to write about a recent experience, and she filled two pages on her preparations for the academic fair. Her account had flair, though her spelling was very poor.

Ungar's comment: "To prepare this child within two years for college would be a daunting task." On the other hand, she was too young to give up getting her there, he thought. He said that he would recommend admitting her to the school. She'd be in a classroom with normal learners, would get the same homework, but would attend the learning center twice a day for remedial work. "You'd probably start out with Ds, but perhaps—with lots of extra hard work—get up to Cs this year," he predicted.

We felt depressed after Ungar's assessment. "In a way I want to come here, but I also don't want to come here," Maria cried as we drove off down the gravel road. But, after visiting the Ranch School in New Mexico, a very small boarding school for severely learning disabled kids, Maria realized that Solebury was a better option. She liked the idea of mixing again with normal learners, and her teachers, who had written glowing recommendations, thought that she'd be able to compete in the more challenging environment. Chelsea's principal also encouraged us after discussing Maria's transfer with Tom Ungar for an hour over the phone.

Pat McArthur, who had resumed counseling Maria at school, wasn't convinced that a boarding school was the right solution. "She's bound to feel rejected again if you put her there," Pat warned. "Besides, bad things can happen at boarding schools." She thought that I should hang in there, but Maria's frequent refrain, "I just can't live with you," was persuasive. After our last court hearing at the end of April, we were left to our own devices, especially after Dr. Casey got a new job and couldn't work with us any longer. Maria objected to finding a new therapist. We had a long, hot summer stretching before us, and I kept my fingers crossed that Solebury would be our solution for the fall. Maria, ever the Catholic, prayed fervently that she would get in. In fact, she became so adamant about the transfer that I worried how she'd survive a rejection.

But then, at the end of May, we received the longed-for phone call. We danced around the kitchen, and then Maria commandeered the phone to let the whole world know, "I've been accepted!" I kept chanting in the background, "Maria got accepted, Maria got accepted!" until my euphoria got on her nerves.

That summer of her sixteenth year was dominated by two ambitions—a job and a driver's license. At school she had received kudos for organizing driver's ed, but the practice of driving was a nightmare since she often confused right with left, and our Honda's stick shift added yet another challenge. I paid for dozens of private lessons, and, whenever she practiced with our car on country roads, I sat next to her shaking like a leaf. By the end of the summer, after flunking the first time, she got her license, and thereafter we argued at least once a day over when and for how long she could borrow the car.

To find a job, we walked one Saturday the length of Wheaton Plaza, our nearest mall. We collected applications and filled them out over lunch. When Maria returned the one to Spencer's, a gift shop, they hired her right then and there. Among her friends, she was the only one who had a job. Everyone else was hoping for a slot on the mayor's youth employment program. Jobs were scarce that summer, even for college kids.

Maria started on a Monday, and, when I picked her up in the evening, she was elated by the business of her day. "All of a sudden we had a hundred customers in the store," she reported breathlessly. She did overtime on her first day, and was asked to work a nine-hour shift on the next. But she was part time, often didn't get called in for days, and then only for a few hours. She easily made friends with her co-workers, liked the silly, goofy, grotesque, slightly obscene merchandise, and enjoyed flirting with the young men who came to buy trinkets for their girlfriends or garish posters for their rooms.

Years later, after she had married him, Maria told me that Simo had been one of the steady customers at Spencer's. I imagine them grinning at each other over barely disguised penises serving as nutcrackers, or boobs flapping from gift bags. After returning a few times, he got her name and number and probably was one of the young men who kept calling, usually hanging up when I answered the phone.

Simo was just one of several young men who wanted more than friendly smiles. Since time immemorial, females like Maria have felt flattered, excited, and anxious as they sense the sexual implications of the young men's overtures. At the time, I was clueless, but in retrospect I can see how her confusion played out on the night before she was to leave for Apple Farm, the arts and music camp.

She had been looking forward to an encore of last summer's happy participation in the band, at the studio, and on the soccer field. She had kept in touch with some campers through a winter reunion in Philadelphia and would be a CIT—a counselor in training—this year, assisting an art teacher in a class for eight-year-olds. She was all packed, and we would leave early the next morning for the long drive to New Jersey.

When she returned late that night from Spencer's, she plunked herself into the lounger in my bedroom, announcing, "I can't stand this house. I need to get away. Need to get away from DC. Someone has been following me for the last three days," she shouted between sobs. "I can't stand it any longer." Dumbfounded, I crouched closer, reaching out to touch her.

"Don't touch me," she screamed. "You and I are just roommates. We have nothing to say to each other. I need to get away."

Well, great, she was about to leave for camp, I argued, she'd be safe there for four weeks. Whoever had followed her would lose track. And, in fact, if she felt that desperate, I'd drive her to Apple Farm in the middle of the night and we'd just sit in the driveway until the morning. "No," she screamed, "I need to get away!" As she moved toward the door, I threatened to call the police, and, when she didn't slow down, I started dialing 911. Outraged, she wrestled the phone from me. "No, not the police!"

We ended up in the bathroom, where I rummaged through the medicine chest and then offered *Baldriantropfen*, an old-time German herbal remedy with calming effects—if you were a believer. "What's in it?" she asked suspiciously when I rolled two capsules onto her palm. We read the label, I translated, and reluctantly she swallowed. She went into her room and closed the door, leaving me to watch the sliver of light on the threshold. When it went off, I tried to sleep for a few hours before we hit the turnpike to New Jersey.

"Maria settled into camp immediately," wrote Kendra and Sharon, the two bushy-tailed counselors from Scotland. "She is full of energy and excitement. She's getting on really well in the bunk and making many, many friends. Her teddy bears are making many friends as well. She is playing lots of soccer and really enjoying her classes. She is thriving in the CIT program. She loves spending time with the small kids here, and they have really taken to her as a role model. She is a joy to have in the bunk."

I sighed with relief, but also wondered whether we were talking about the same Maria who had threatened to run off only a week earlier. A role model to younger girls—they must be kidding! And this, despite the fact that Maria had made no effort to hide her shady past.

"Seems that you've been through a rough year," said the camp director, a middle-aged woman who made her rounds on a little tractor and stopped long enough to say hello. Among the thousands of campers this woman had met, Maria stood out. It hadn't taken much prompting for Maria to cheerfully volunteer the résumé of her past year: running off with a man, getting arrested for shoplifting, spending time in jail and a shelter. Maria took your breath away as you watched her ride the roller coaster of her yin and yang. As she zoomed up and down, she waved to her stunned audience, and her smiling candor just warmed your heart.

She had another great Apple experience that summer, playing trumpet and saxophone in different bands, painting props for a musical, organizing a soccer tournament, and flirting with another CIT from New York.

I came for parents' day halfway through the four-week session and brought houseguests from Vienna along. Maria awaited us at the gate with, "What took you so long?" She desperately needed a break from rural bliss and demanded that we take her to the nearest mega mall. It seemed that lots of other campers needed the mall fix as well. Wherever we sat, whenever we turned a corner, Apple Farm kids waved an enthusiastic hello. Little girls from the drawing class in which Maria assisted as CIT squealed when they spotted her and ran over for a kiss and a cuddle. Maria indulged them with an air of "I just can't help being so very popular."

"I tuck them in at night and read them bedtime stories," she informed me. "Some of them are really homesick and need extra cuddles." By summer's end, her little charges voted her "most dedicated CIT."

I felt touched by my daughter's compassion, and, when a postcard arrived three days after our visit, thanking us for making the seven-hour round-trip, I wrote in my diary, "There's a possibility that we may survive the rest of the summer without a major fiasco."

We did. And finally the day arrived to load our brand-new Honda with all the things printed on the school list, including the favorite blanket with its Coca-Cola slogan and the black Sears trunk I'd hauled around during long-ago graduate student days.

The girls' dorm at Solebury was abuzz with the shrieks and laughter of reunions when we hauled our stuff into a bare-boards room. Maria took one look at her assigned roommate and decided that she wouldn't like her—a feeling that seemed mutual. She ogled the sisterhood of athletic black girls, and, for the next two years would work hard to become part of their circle. At Solebury, as elsewhere, she was a minority, and growing up in predominately black DC had shaped the preference for her alliances.

After Maria settled into the room, the friendly den mother explained house rules, including a curfew of eleven o'clock. Maria groaned, rolled her eyes, and then dismissed me with a casual wave. I felt elation all the way home. For the first time in fifteen years, I wondered how I might like to spend my evenings. Within a week, I sang in the church choir, joined a book group, and read stories to inner-city kids in an after-school program.

I established an 800-number that enabled Maria to call home easily, and wrote to her every other day. The pay phone in her dorm was often busy, and, when I did get through, a friendly soul had to retrieve Maria, who was often "roomed" for breaking house rules.

"I was trying to wash the outside of the door, not realizing it was past eleven," she'd explain. "I was just outside checking on the weather," she said another time, caught after curfew.

I tried to sound sympathetic when listening to these colossal misunderstandings, but inwardly rejoiced that now a whole institution was dealing with my child's obstinate, stubborn, sneaky, and uncooperative behavior. This was worth every penny of the $27,500 tuition, I figured, even if it would send me to the poorhouse. My girl needed discipline and structure, wake-up calls in the morning and lights out at night, rigorous exercise followed by mandatory study hall, tests that monitored true progress, deadlines set in stone, and chores to be completed, no matter what. For once, I couldn't be blamed for failure—or so I thought.

I had just mailed a winter jacket against first snow flurries when I received a telephoned message: "Don't write or call me anymore. You lie and double cross me, and I don't want to have anything to do with you!" *What was all that about?* I wondered, and called Dr. Casey for some insight.

"Seems that she feels abandoned again," Dr. Casey diagnosed matter-of-factly, implying, "What did you think you were doing when you dropped the child off at that boarding school?" And hadn't Pat McArthur predicted that Maria would feel abandoned? Guilt-tripping, I was very meek when next we connected, and Maria expounded on the pain and disappointments of her wretched life: her soccer team had lost 4–0; her knee was hurting again; she needed medication for her cramps; and she'd had to drop math to Algebra II, and Spanish to level one. "Send me my comforter," she said and hung up before I could promise to mail it.

Four weeks later, I drove to Solebury for the first parent-teachers conference, to be followed by a long weekend at home. Maria was upset that she'd had to drop to remedial classes and receive low grades after As and Bs and high achievement at Chelsea. But her counselor and teachers told me that she was adjusting to school life. For the past week she hadn't even been "roomed." Among the group of incoming students, several—like the German girl we had already invited for Thanksgiving—wouldn't make it to the end of the semester. The blond waif had been caught smoking a reefer in the woods, and the two DC-area boys, who repeatedly sneaked alcohol into the dorm, had also been expelled. Solebury had a fair process for reviewing infractions, and Maria soon got to know the protocol, maintaining tenure a few times by the skin of her teeth.

The week before my first parent/teachers conference, Maria had told me that she wouldn't ride home with me. She would take the train, she said, and spend the weekend with Dee. Who was Dee?

"Never mind," she hissed, but then ended up sitting grumpily in the car next to me. Once home, she hogged the phone, calling everyone, including Jackie, the manager at Spencer's, who offered Maria a few hours of work.

Jackie, a middle-aged, petite, and spunky woman, liked Maria and looked out for her. Maria often helped Jackie close the store and count the cash. Sometimes, between $20 and $30 would be missing, and I worried that Maria, who was allowed to operate the register, caused imbalances by transposing numbers when she rang up a sale. She was likely to punch $12, instead of $21. Once, when she was nine, she insisted that the year had 356 days, "I bet you five dollars." Stubborn insistence often compounded her handicap.

With Jackie across the table, Maria counted and recounted nickels and dimes, sometimes past midnight. Eventually, they'd discover an error or let it go, then would stop at Burger King for a double Whopper before Jackie dropped Maria off on her way home.

From what I gathered bit by bit, Jackie was the head of a dysfunctional household, settled way off in the boonies. Her ex-husband slept on the couch, her adult children were in and out, and her father-in-law was about to die. In fact, everyone hoped he would do so soon so they could sell the house, split the profit, and move down south. Meanwhile, Jackie was holding forth at Spencer's, with Maria her steady confidant. When I saw Jackie at Thanksgiving, she was sporting a pricey sweat suit with Solebury emblem, purchased at the campus store through the credit line I had established for pencils and erasers. "I'll pay you back," Maria promised vaguely when I raised an eyebrow. I promptly limited future purchases and decided that Jackie owed me.

So, when Maria announced that Jackie had invited her for an overnight during the Christmas break, I had a long talk with the woman, making sure she understood her responsibilities in hosting a minor. Jackie promised proper conduct and, admittedly, looked cute in her Solebury outfit. *I'd like one too*, I thought.

Maria returned from her Jackie outing reeking of tobacco, in need of sleep, but in a jolly mood. "We played poker all night, and I won," she said, throwing a fistful of coins onto the kitchen table. Everyone had gotten into the act—grandpa, the ex, the new boyfriend, adult children, and their friends, Maria reported. They cheered Maria's savvy and good luck, and she felt grand being the youngest in the gambling gang.

By summer, grandpa had died and Jackie and her clan were ready to sell, pack up, and move. Maria helped pack and then called from a strip motel where the group had settled for the night. "Pleeeze," could she stay with Jackie, she pleaded. I talked to Jackie, who assured me that all was good and right. Next, they were all going to stay in a tent on a campground because Jackie needed a few more paychecks before trucking to South Carolina. "Pleeeze, Mom, pleeeze let me stay with them, it will be so much fun," Maria begged.

I said no, and was about to be ignored, when the heavens opened with torrential rains that also washed away the area's happy campsites. Jackie disappeared without farewells, but let Maria know her whereabouts. Three years later, Maria, newly wed to Simo, caught a ride to South Carolina in search of Jackie. She found Jackie settled in a trailer, with the ex still sleeping on the couch, and both of them working at a diner down the road. "Jackie said that I could stay and work with them," Maria reported, but then decided to return to husband Simo in Virginia.

If the relationship with Jackie set me on edge, I felt truly blessed by the support of the Logan family during the Solebury years. Reyna Logan was from Colombia and had come to the United States as an exchange student. She and Maria felt an instant bond because of a shared heritage. Reyna and her husband had two bright and beautiful daughters, one a year older and one a year younger than Maria. Our girls had become friends during rites of passage at All Souls, and, as luck would have it, the Logans moved to Pennsylvania a year before Maria arrived at Solebury and lived only twenty-five minutes from the campus. Maria was a welcome addition to the family, Reyna assured me, and I gladly signed the permission slip for weekends with the Logans. They were involved in a Unitarian fellowship, and Maria didn't object to attending Sunday services with the girls. Before Thanksgiving, the family was going to fast and eat nothing but a bowl of rice at the end of the day, "So we can experience what it's like for most people in this world," Maria explained.

"Hurrah, she's taking our values seriously," I wrote into my diary. "I feel sooo grateful! The universe is looking out for me. I can abdicate, Reyna is taking over!"

And for a while she did. She'd pick up Maria sometime on Saturday and load the heavy schoolbag and laundry hamper into the trunk. They'd return to Solebury on Sunday night, always in a mad dash over the hills and through the woods with both of them holding their breath wondering whether Reyna, notoriously late, would make it by seven, the mandatory time for weekend returns.

Friends visit Maria at Solebury

From what I could gather, Maria was a good houseguest who participated in chores, folded her laundry, and studied and partied with the girls. She secretly admired Marie, the oldest sister, who participated in many extra-curricular activities, despite her dependence on a wheelchair. Marie was an excellent student who aimed at medical school, and she was the soul of a group of seniors who enjoyed hanging out at the house. Marie arranged gigantic slumber parties, and, for weeks before the prom, she fixed dates and hairstyles and advised on makeup and couture. She was a dedicated friend with a commanding presence, and Maria watched her like a mesmerized rabbit, wanting to be just like Marie.

Academically, that was impossible. Though Maria had survived the first trimester with passing grades in her remedial courses, chemistry and English soon did her in. By February, she was about to fail.

"I don't know why it's so hard for me to ask for help," she wailed during her break at home. "If I could ask for help, I could really make it." Ellen, who had come to visit, listened quietly to Maria's litany of failure, and later observed, "She owns her LD for the first time, and that's a bitter experience. Let's see what she'll make of it."

I couldn't help her with chemistry, but for English I read a number of plays onto a tape, since Maria found printed dialogue perplexing. It took me three-and-a-half hours to read *Pygmalion*, all the while thinking that the witty-wordy George Bernard Shaw could use some editing. The ordeal, however, was worth it, because Maria ended up writing the best paper on the play's underlying social criticism. In math she zigzagged between As and Ds. She ended the year with a C- in math, an F in chemistry, but a very encouraging C+ in learning skills. For her outstanding work in the Native American philosophy course, she got an A and a prize.

The dean suggested that Maria repeat eleventh grade to prepare her better for the academic rigors of the colleges that Solebury's students were likely to attend. The dean's proposal threw us for a loop. I had planned to retire within a year and move to Seattle, and Maria was itching to finish high school and get on with the rest of her life. We both found the prospect of an added year at Solebury thoroughly depressing.

13.

"POMP AND CIRCUMSTANCE"

After a flurry of phone calls and consultations, Maria returned to Solebury in September as a senior after all.

"She just has to graduate next spring," advised the leader of my Latin American parents support group, a psychologist and the challenged mom of three children adopted from Latin America. Over the years, she had patiently listened to the ups and downs of raising Maria. "Holding Maria back a year will only prolong opportunities for rebellion," observed my friend. "She'd be likely to drop out and not finish at all."

Next, I called Art Randall, Maria's learning skills teacher, who was alarmed at the suggestion that Maria repeat eleventh grade. "Given her age [she was seventeen], I would never recommend that Maria repeat eleventh grade," Art said. "I think she would be miserable having to spend two more years at Solebury. Her self-confidence has been improving, and she should be encouraged to graduate next year and then continue from there. She improved a lot last year, and there is every indication that she will continue to do so."

Finally, I talked to the school's academic dean, who wasn't convinced that graduating Maria next year was a good decision. She wouldn't be sufficiently prepared for a four-year college, he warned. However, he wouldn't stand in the way of a high school diploma, if that was our goal.

"Yippee, I'm a senior," rejoiced Maria, almost jumping to the ceiling. She'd graduate with former and current classmates, marching down that grassy path to the sounds of "Pomp and Circumstance." As far as college was concerned, well, she wasn't sure whether she wanted to pursue academics. All things considered, it looked as if our life was back on track.

With Maria safely at Solebury, I seized the opportunity to attend a conference in Buenos Aires, Argentina, at the end of September. The USIA-sponsored symposium focused on strengthening democratic institutions to create better-functioning civil societies around the world. At the time, I was editor of USIA's newly created electronic journal on democracy and human rights, available worldwide over the Internet. A special issue had helped prepare for the Buenos Aires conference.

Sending me to Argentina was, in part, a reward for my survival of fierce battles with policy officers who objected to liberal views expressed in the journal's academic content. In *Bowling Alone*, Robert D. Putnam, for example, saw how the erosion of civic engagement in the United States was posing a threat to the country's democratic institutions, while Seymour Martin Lipset maintained in *Malaise and Resiliency* that America's civic institutions were still robust and thriving. In their zeal to spread democracy throughout the world, some policy officers didn't appreciate a presentation of critical debate within the United States. It seemed that we had moved light-years away from Ed Murrow's dictum of "telling America's story, warts and all."

With backing from department heads, we usually prevailed after making small editorial adjustments, but I felt exhausted and bruised. "Take a break and enjoy yourself at the conference," advised my editor in chief as she signed the travel orders.

Maria and Solebury were informed of my upcoming one-week absence. Maria had permission to spend the weekend with the Logans, and, in case of an emergency, Ellen would mother her long distance. Before I left, Ellen met me at Chico's, the upscale clothing store at Union Station, to help me pick a suitable outfit, and then added a lovely necklace to complete my new look. "Don't worry and have a good time," she said with a hug.

My sister Claudia came from Vancouver, Canada, to share my room at the Sheraton in Buenos Aires, and, while I was very preoccupied with filing news stories about the conference for USIA's press service, she explored the city and environs and reported back over breakfast. "All the women are young and gorgeous," she observed, "except the mothers on Plaza de Mayo." Claudia had watched them on the city's most historic square on a Thursday afternoon. Heads covered with white kerchiefs, they'd been silently marching for years to call attention to the disappearance of their children during the government's military reign from 1976 to 1983.

During taxi rides between the hotel and conference center, I noticed that Buenos Aires looked more like Paris than other Latin American cities with their heritage of Spanish colonialism. Buenos Aires had broad boulevards, groomed parks, *fin-de-siècle* architecture, and its residents looked European. One evening we ventured to La Boca, a picturesque and shabby neighborhood, where the slithering tango was born. After supper we enjoyed a show of passionate dance and soulful song at one of those seedy bars that cater to tourists.

The conference over, we spent our last day together on a motorboat that meandered through the Rio Plata's tentacle of canals, dropping off schoolchildren and groceries as we passed grand mansions and colorful shacks built on stilts. Along the way, I bought a plump tan leather backpack for my budding scholar at Solebury.

Returning on a Saturday, I had barely walked into the front door when Solebury's student dean called to tell me that Maria had been suspended for two school days and was on her way home. The previous weekend she had signed herself out to the Logans, and, returning late on Sunday night, had mumbled something about going to the museum in Philadelphia and then getting locked in when it closed. That sounded pretty fishy, and, when Maria was asked to appear before the judiciary committee, she quickly confessed that she had spent the weekend in DC, the forbidden city.

"She arrived home loaded with anger," I reported in my diary. "On Monday night she sneaked out of the house and spent the night with some man. I'm disgusted. I really want her out of my hair. Can't wait to get away. She'll have to fend for herself. She'll find ways to blame me for her rotten life, and my knee-jerk reactions are no help in resolving our problems. She knows how to make me feel lousy."

Maria returned to Solebury knowing that she couldn't afford another infraction lest she be sent home for good. One of her peer advisors and fellow classmates was Kazu, a student from Japan. A year younger and about twenty years wiser than Maria, he was one of two students on the four-member judiciary committee. Maria invited him to come home with her for Thanksgiving, his first of several stays at our house. "Who's coming for dinner?" she asked when I picked them up at the station. "Let's show Kazu a real family affair." With the excuse of a cold, she then plunked herself in front of the TV and never lifted a finger as I scrambled to invite four extras to round out our Thanksgiving affair. Luckily, I liked Kazu instantly, and he followed me around like a puppy.

As soon as he had unpacked, he asked me if I could teach him German over Thanksgiving. He had brought a German grammar and felt confident that he could learn the language in two weeks. Sorry, I said, I couldn't possibly teach him that fast. He was disappointed, and then told me how he had learned English almost overnight. When he arrived in this country, his English was rudimentary, and so he decided that he wouldn't read or speak another word of Japanese before becoming fluent in English, even if Japanese fellow students at Solebury were tempting him to use his mother tongue. He succeeded within weeks, skipped a grade, and was acing chemistry and the sciences.

While he made cranberry sauce and chopped vegetables for our Thanksgiving dinner, he told me about life back home. "There were about fifty students in my grade, and all we ever did was memorize information and then feed it back to the teacher. I had read that students in America discuss everything and have dialogues with their teachers, and so I badgered my parents to let me study here," Kazu recalled. His parents finally relented, though sending their only child to high school in America presented a great financial hardship. No, he wasn't homesick. "My parents are old," he explained with a dismissive gesture. "They don't really understand me. Our apartment in Tokyo is very small and cramped; not like this house."

Right then it occurred to me that Maria could be sitting at a kitchen table in Tokyo, explaining, "My mother is quite old and doesn't really understand me. I really hated school. We live in this big old house, but I really prefer cozy apartments like yours." As Kazu raked leaves in the yard, loved the food I cooked, asked politely what time he should be home before heading to a trendy bookstore on Connecticut Avenue, I wondered whether my grouchy, obstinate Maria could possibly turn into a charming houseguest in Tokyo. *I bet she could; she usually charms everyone, except her mother,* I thought. And Kazu, whom I was ready to adopt, might just be a real pain in the neck back home. These teenagers need recycling, I decided. Exchange them and then everyone would be happy!

Meanwhile, Maria said she was in pain. After two arthroscopies, her knee was still aching, despite dozens of therapy sessions. The pain had steadily increased during the soccer season as she participated with her usual passion for the game. Aspirin didn't seem to be the solution, and we were casting about for alternative treatments when I learned of Dr. Li, a Chinese doctor who healed through acupuncture. He practiced in Maryland, an hour's drive from downtown DC, and getting an appointment took a while. When we finally got there, the rumors of his popularity were confirmed. His waiting room was overflowing with the rejects of traditional medicine, and timidly we joined the hopeful crowd. With a young doctor at his side, Dr. Li hustled between different rooms to administer his needles. He uttered few words in English and some grunts in Chinese, and then declared, after a brief examination, that Maria would be kicking again after ten sessions. We signed on and I watched her flinch when the good doctor positioned a dozen needles along the meridians at her knee. Skipping from the office afterwards, she observed, "I think this may work. I feel much lighter."

Driving her to the sessions meant taking off almost half a day at work, and I soon let Maria drive, hoping that she could eventually find her own way. Negotiating the beltway and highways was difficult, also because of her poor sense of direction. So, when Kazu visited, I suggested that he help her get there. Off they went in our snow-white Honda, the first car I'd ever bought brand new. And then the highway trooper called.

"Your daughter just rammed the divider on the Dulles access road. She's fine, so is the other kid. But the car has to be towed."

"Can I talk to my daughter, please?" I asked, alarmed.

"Mom, I'm so sorry. I don't know what happened," she cried.

"I'm glad you and Kazu are okay," I said, barely hiding my fury over the wrecked car. While I made arrangements for car and kids to be towed, I received a call from a taxi driver who had watched the accident unfold.

"I was driving behind her. She wasn't going fast at all. But the highway was wet, and suddenly she seemed to lose control and veered off the pavement and hit the metal barrier. I stopped, and she was crying, 'My mother is going to kill me.' I told her that I'd call you first chance I got and tell you that she wasn't driving recklessly." Everyone at the office said how lucky that the kids were unscathed, and I nodded in a daze.

The rest of that Thanksgiving disappeared into a blur. I got the flu and went to bed. Maria moved out and stayed with friends I didn't know. Kazu helped himself to leftovers in the fridge. The insurance company called to let me know that my Honda, at less than 26,000 miles, couldn't be repaired. Once the house was quiet, I realized that the kids had left. For different reasons, they didn't bother to say good-bye. It took me another week to recover from the flu—and from life.

Maria returned three weeks later announcing, "I've grown up a lot. There is such a thing as growing up." It was music to my ears, and, for the first half of that Christmas vacation, she was friendly. Shopping and going to work without a car had been exhausting, and we had a low-key celebration without a tree. But, just before year's end, we bought a secondhand Honda and were back in the hospitality business for dinner with friends on New Year's Day. Nineteen ninety-seven would bring us momentous changes. Maria would turn eighteen, graduate from high school, and be on her own, while I would turn sixty, retire, and move to Seattle. We both felt excited and apprehensive.

"Maria was nice during the first week," I wrote in my diary. "But during the second week, she became her ugly, screaming, defiant self again. And now she has been gone for twenty-four hours, and I don't know where she is. I feel helpless, anxious, fed up, angry. I called Spencer's this morning and talked to Gina, whom I know by name. She said that Maria had spent the night with her, not to worry. But now it is 10:00 p.m. and I still haven't heard. Maria called last night, and we agreed on a midnight curfew, and then she just didn't show up."

I didn't see her for the next three days, and nobody would or could tell me where she was. On Sunday, she was to return to Solebury, and, before heading to church, I left money for the fare and her January allowance on the kitchen table. When I called home in the early afternoon, Maria answered in tears. She had a terrible rash and couldn't go to school, she said. "You are going," I countered, "I don't want to see you when I get home." Sure enough, money and Maria were gone when I returned, but at 10:30 p.m., Solebury reported her missing. When I called home on Monday afternoon, Maria answered and promised to stay. Checking her over, I noticed pale remnants of a rash. My guess was that the outbreak had something to do with schoolwork left undone over the holidays. I decided to take the next day off to drive her to Solebury.

We had a conference with the friendly student dean who accepted my note, asking to excuse Maria's absence for health reasons. In another note, I stipulated that she not come home until the end of the trimester in February. That night, I slept like a babe. I also knew that I needed professional help and called on Celia Gardner, whose parenting classes I had attended. Celia listened and took notes as I rehashed my wretched history of mothering Maria. "You need to establish firm boundaries and give her clear options," Celia advised. "Call me the next time you're about to cave in. I want to be your sponsor."

The upshot of sessions with Celia was my letter to Maria. It makes me sound amazingly clearheaded, despite the muddles of my heart.

Wednesday, January 14, 97

Dear Maria Consuelo:

It was good to hear from you last night that you have caught up with some of your schoolwork. I am sorry that your lungs still feel sore, and I hope you will get better soon. Perhaps the Spectrabiotics and algae, due to arrive today, will help in battling the health problem.

As for your birthday, I would be glad to visit you and help you celebrate, weather permitting. I could arrive on Friday eve., spend the night and most of Saturday with you. I would have to leave Saturday eve., so I could sing Sunday morning in the choir. Let me know whether you would like me to visit.

The next time I see you, you will be 18. That means that you have choices from here on:

1. One of your choices is not to come back home. If you choose that, you are on your own.

2. The other choice is to live at home during your breaks from school and treat me with respect and consideration while you live at home.

Let me just recap the recent history of your behavior that leads me to write this letter and outline your choices.

The end of your stay at Thanksgiving was so awful that I suggested you spend your Christmas vacation somewhere else. I dreaded your return. You arrived before Christmas, saying that you had grown up a lot and that, no matter what, we would have a good Christmas. We did, and I was especially thrilled that you had bought three presents for me and had taken great pains to find the right kind of black vest.

But then I noticed that you did none of your papers or homework, you started yelling at me, and became frantic when your social life didn't turn out as you wanted it. On Thursday you went out. On the phone you agreed to come home at midnight. You did not return until Saturday when you changed your clothes and disappeared again until Monday, thus missing a day and a half of school. On reflection, I should not have written the note to excuse your absence because you were not at home when you were sick. I realize that I have to stop rescuing you. You have to learn to accept responsibility for your actions and bear the consequences.

You tell me that you hate Solebury. Well, you hate being at home when you are at home. And after a few days at Spencer's, you hate Spencer's. You hated Chelsea and were desperate to get to Solebury. No matter what your feelings are about the school, you are there to get an education. That should be a priority on your agenda. You did outstanding work during the last trimester, and I am confident that you can do well again.

At Solebury, you are surrounded by teachers, advisors, and administrators who want you to succeed. They like you and are rooting for you. Accept what they can offer! I understand that you are homesick for the city, but you are back in the city at least every four weeks!

If you stick it out, I will continue to support you on the rocky climb of higher education. College and learning will always be difficult for you because of your handicap. However, you have a God-given superior intelligence and outstanding talents. You've got the stuff to surmount your problems, if you set your mind to it. Instead of thinking that the world owes you and revolves around you, start thinking what you can offer to the world: a friendly manner, a compassionate heart, a keen intellect, a great sense of humor, reliable work habits, and a deep sense of what's right and just.

If you choose to quit, you will be unskilled and unschooled and you will end up in a quagmire of economic hardship with no professional opportunities.

This is a very important time in your life, and your choices will determine your future.

I hope and pray that you will choose the right course.

As for myself, I refuse to continue to be abused and battered by you. That is my choice: I can refuse to live with your inconsiderate behavior. You have no idea what anxieties you cause when you disappear! I worry about your safety, I cannot sleep, I cannot concentrate on my work the next day, and I feel physically and emotionally exhausted. From now on, I do not need to live with your mistreatment. You are a young adult, and, if you want to, you can be on your own!

Love, Mom

When I called a few days later, a subdued Maria said that yes, she'd like me to come to Solebury for her birthday on January 24. And so I took Friday afternoon off, and drove north on Interstate 95 through sheets of rain, and then slithered along country roads over melting ice and snow.

She was in the gym, keeping score at a basketball game, when I picked her up. She wore high heels with the dark brown sweater and tight pants I had sent in a birthday package. She was a stunning eighteen-year-old, all Ms. Officious as she passed the scoreboard to a classmate. Accompanied by a chorus of "have a good time, Maria," we exited for our outing.

The Washington-slept-here type of inn I had chosen for our overnight sat right next to the canal, whose waters stood at a precarious level. After skipping and jumping through puddles and over snow banks, we settled for supper right next to a roaring fire, and, once our waitress had been briefed on the importance of the day, she served dessert with birthday candles and stayed to chat. On our best behavior, we looked elegant and were aware that the evening marked Maria's passage into adulthood as well as shifts in our mother-daughter equation. To mark the event and indulge in some nostalgia, I wore the red Calvin Klein sweater into which I had wrapped my little girl over sixteen years ago when I had brought her home from Colombia.

I thought that, at eighteen, Maria should own the tidbits that documented her precarious beginnings, so, back in our room, I presented her with a shoe box full of adoption papers and the little outfit she had worn when I had first met her. Maria looked at the box's content without curiosity or enthusiasm, but, years later, I learned that she took it to her next therapy session.

"We spread out the jumper and tiny jersey and rubber pants, the socks and the little blue sandals," her counselor recalled. "And then I said, 'I wonder what the little girl was like who wore this outfit.' We spent the whole hour thinking about that toddler." During the many moves of her young adult life, Maria lost just about everything she ever owned, but the blue sandals—her beloved *zapatos*—sat on the windowsill of the Florida cottage, where she had spent her last happy months.

There was no TV at our inn, as Maria immediately noted with a groan, and, for the rest of the evening, we listened to the downpour and watched the rising waters outside our window. While I curled up with a good read, Maria pulled out a paper on Colombia that had been growing into a forty-page tome. Her learning skills teacher had assigned the topic to teach independent research and, making use of resources in the library and over the Internet, Maria had accumulated her birth country's history of war and more war, and then some mayhem. Her class on Latin American history provided an additional framework for research and fed her growing passion for human rights and social justice.

Months later, when spring break rolled around, I suggested that we visit Latin America as an early graduation present. "Would you like to go to Colombia?" I asked her, thinking that I could probably enlist help from colleagues in Bogota to make the trip a safe experience. Better not go there at this time, my well-informed daughter told me—too many murders and kidnappings. Her caution surprised me. Was she perhaps scared of confronting the traumas of her early childhood?

We went to Guatemala instead. Our connection was Raúl, a radiologist who had stayed with us for six weeks while taking a course at Walter Reed's Institute of Pathology across the street. Like the other ninety-nine radiologists who stayed with us over a ten-year period, Raúl had been included in our family life and the circle of our friends, and Maria liked him especially since he was short, compact, and Latino.

Raúl and his soon-to-be wife Monica met us on arrival, saw to it that we settled in a safe neighborhood, and then immediately whisked Maria off to "ladies night" at their favorite disco. Maria was in heaven! The next day, Raúl had a van pick us up for an outing to Antigua, the former colonial capital. While lunching in the courtyard of an elegant hotel, we watched two colorful parrots devour papayas on a swinging feeder. The parrots later dominated Maria's most mature drawing, a complex piece of art with yin-yang symbols, a lush leafy foreground, and a double bench facing a barren tree at the horizon. It's framed and hanging on the wall next to my computer. Every time I look, it invites me to discover new details as I try to decipher the young artist's intent and feelings.

On our trip, she let me know her feelings loud and clear. She was more interested in discoing than sightseeing, she said, and tolerated our excursion to the famous Mayan pyramids at Tikal only because one of our guides was rather cute. After an evening hike through the jungle under a brilliant starry sky, she didn't return to our room once lights were out. The next morning she hinted that she'd spent the night out in the open with that cute guide, and shamelessly complained about mosquito bites "all over."

When we explored the highland villages around Lake Atitlán, Maria announced that she'd had it and desperately needed to return to Guatemala City and disco options with Raúl and Monica. Right then, I got violently ill with diarrhea and vomiting and, unable to lift my head from the pillow, gave her money for the bus, with the promise that I would join her as soon as I could. It took me three days to recover, and, when I arrived at our hotel in the city, I found Maria holed up with a box of crackers in front of the TV. It was the middle of the week, and our friends had been too busy to indulge her.

Maria was her hostile, grumpy self by the time we arrived for departure at the airport. "I'd rather live here than there," she said wistfully as we waited. Next to us was an American couple, rocking a Guatemalan baby. They were surrounded by North American baby paraphernalia—stroller, pampers, formula, infant seat, and toys for the little prince, who might have been found abandoned in some doorway.

"Look," I nudged Maria, "they're adopting."

She took in the scene and hissed, "Adoption is wrong. Children should not be given away, but stay in their home country."

I didn't know whether I wanted to laugh or cry. Had I really raised this slouching brat who denounced the good fortune of privilege and opportunity while jetting around the world, decked out in designer labels from eyeglasses to Nike high-tops, exuding the sophistication of a New England boarding school education that came with a price tag beyond our means?

She really could use one of those spankings, administered some fifty years ago with that-will-teach-you admonitions, I thought. Knowing better, I turned to the radiant couple, and, for a few moments, shared with them the joys of adoptive parenthood. Wasn't their little boy simply perfect, we marveled, and weren't they so very lucky to take him home. I spared them an introduction to the hostile and confused teenager who glared at us from afar.

However, Guatemala reverberated. When a youth group at our church planned a trip to Guatemala at the end of the school year, Maria signed up with alacrity. Our young people were to work in a rural community where a Catholic priest from Minnesota had worked for thirty years establishing agricultural co-ops. His involvement attracted many volunteers who assisted in the infirmary or classrooms, in the coffee plantations, and with beekeeping. Would she perhaps like to stay in the village for a year and really get immersed in Latin American life, language, and culture, I asked Maria. The idea started percolating in her brain. "I think I'll be volunteering in Guatemala after graduation," she'd say to friends, trying it out for size, enjoying "wow" responses.

At school, she concentrated on her studies with unprecedented vigor. "I think I finally know how to study and ask for help," Maria observed. Since study hall was too distracting, she was allowed to use an empty classroom, where she often burned midnight oil. "She's been working like a dog," her Latin American history teacher told me at the last parents' conference of that senior year. "And I can always count on her participation in lively discussions," he reported. For her senior project, Maria chose to work in her former pre-school in Adams Morgan, the heart of Washington's Hispanic community. During a student assembly, Maria showed off photos she had taken of her little charges and talked about her experience with passion and compassion. "She's a leader with a big heart," her teacher observed.

That spring, Maria also made good money planting Christmas trees on a farm near Solebury. She crouched for hours putting seedlings into the moist earth, drove the tractor between jobs, got all muddy, soaked, and tanned, and was "the best kid I've ever had working for me," as the farmer told a neighbor. "I think Maria secretly fell in love with the land and country life," Maria's counselor observed. "The city girl discovered deep roots, connecting her to the earth and planting."

Back in DC, I got our house ready for sale. The market was slow and depressed, and it was imperative to make the property look its very best. I found a motley crew of painters who started to apply Maria Theresa Yellow, Austria's imperial color, onto the stucco, with white trim around the windows, and hunter green on the shutters and the front door. It was a big conversion from boring beige and brown, requiring several coats of paint, and the work was often interrupted by bad weather, or the alcoholic stupor of my crew. They were practically living in our yard, and quickly bonded with Magic, our dog. With all the comings and goings, the garden gate stayed mostly open, and Magic discovered a new world out there. She roamed the neighborhood, made friends on the Walter Reed campus, returning only for supper and a good night's sleep. I didn't know what should become of her. My exit plans from DC had no provisions for Magic. "Get rid of her, Mom," Maria had advised for years. After the initial euphoria of owning a dog, Maria complained about Magic's bad manners and odor from her chronic skin disease. Magic needed a heavy dose of cortisone and frequent veterinary care. "Get rid of her," was Maria's frequent refrain. "Get another dog!" But I had remained loyal to Magic for seven years. Now we were nearing the end of our DC tenure, and I wondered what would become of her, especially as she acted out of control. When I locked the gates on weekends or caged her in the basement, Magic managed to chew her way out, often bleeding in the process.

And then one night, she stayed away. I called the area's pounds for days, but nobody had seen her. After a week, I received a call from a pound some ten miles away, requesting that I pick her up. I asked two neighbors to come along.

The veterinarian at the pound wanted to know why this dog was on the loose. After listening to my saga, she concluded, "It seems this dog is a burden to you. You'd do better having her put to sleep." I started to cry, realizing that she was right. Leaving the leather leash on the counter, I walked away, and my neighbors joined me crying all the way home.

I called Maria.

"Magic is gone."

"Let her go, Mom. She's useless anyway."

"You don't understand, Maria. I had her put to sleep."

"Oh, no," she cried, bursting into violent sobs that shook the airwaves.

Despite her careless talk, her dog's death affected Maria deeply. She asked for photos, saved condolence cards from classmates, and eulogized Magic in the yearbook.

That full-page yearbook statement climaxed a weekend of graduation celebrations on the coldest day of June "for the hottest class ever," as John Brown, the head of Solebury, observed. Parents, siblings, friends, and teachers sat shivering on white folding chairs while the class of '97 marched down that grassy path to the sounds of Elgar's "Pomp and Circumstance." As the alphabet would have it, my radiant Maria was paired with a solemn Kazu, and, when I stepped into the path to snap their photo, the image was all blurry from my tears.

Maria had missed honor roll by a fraction of one point, but John Brown noted her extraordinary achievement when he read the list of winners. Our friends, who filled a whole row, had driven up to New Hope the day before. Many of us, realizing our girl's momentous achievement, sniffled into hankies with joy and wonder, and, in my case, exhaustion.

Instinctively, I knew that Maria was peaking right then and there in front of our very eyes, and we made graduation a most festive affair. There were eight of us overnighting in a stately Victorian bed and breakfast with canopied beds, lacey doilies, and breakfast served on Wedgwood china. For supper, we walked across the Delaware to an old railway station that had been converted into a restaurant that offered nouvelle cuisine. During dessert, Maria passed around her yearbook, opened to her entry. From the roll of portraits a local photographer had taken, Maria had chosen one with an enigmatic Mona Lisa smile. In her long statement, she thanked family and friends by name, and, as the book went around the table, everyone was touched.

"Oh Maria," cried Ellen, wrapping my beaming child into her arms. "Very nice," said Nancy with a teary crack in her voice as she handed me the book. I read with growing wonder, especially moved by the final paragraphs.

"I would like to thank all the friends that I have made here, and over the years, for all they have done," Maria wrote.

> My greatest thanks to my dog, my mother, my birth parents, and God.
>
> To my dog Magic, I will miss you.
>
> To God, thank you, I would not be here without you.
>
> To my mother, I know I have not been the best kid, but I finally got it together. Thanks for trying so hard to get me, to get it all right and stay on track. Thanks for adopting me and giving me a good home. Thanks for all your love and support.
>
> I thank my birth parents, wherever you are, for giving me life.
>
> Finally, to all who have helped me in this life, I say thanks.

The last sentence has since been engraved on a plaque next to a pine tree that was donated by the owner of the Christmas tree farm. Planted near the girls' dormitory, the tree keeps growing and spreading its branches. "I think of Maria whenever I pass the tree," says Peter, her history teacher.

The graduate

14.

GUATEMALA AND OTHER GLITCHES

On a Sunday in June, high school graduates lined up at All Souls Church to be recognized for their accomplishments. One young man was headed to Harvard, another to Swarthmore, and Maria Kreutzer would immerse herself in Hispanic culture by volunteering for a year in Guatemala. Applause. After the service, Maria perched on the stage of the community hall, surrounded by her paintings, drawings, quilts, and gigantic African mask. Parishioners came to review the display and congratulated the beaming artist on her achievement. At home, we invited friends for a farewell party that featured Maria's art with price tags. She sold quite a bit, but the checks barely made it to the bank before hundreds of dollars just evaporated while she was hanging out with friends.

In preparation for the trip, Maria packed duffel bags with a year's supply of shampoo, Tampax, and the little white calcium pills she took to compensate for her lactose intolerance. On June 24, she joined the group of excited All Souls kids under the care of a parent and the assistant minister. The young people would help build clinics in villages in San Lucas near Lake Atitlan, and, when the group left Guatemala after two weeks, Maria would stay and plant trees or help in the clinic and at school. I had talked to Father Greg, the American priest who had been developing these projects, and he promised to keep an eye on Maria.

I dropped her off in a mood of self-congratulation. Hadn't I done a great job getting her there? Hadn't I been attentive to her need to reclaim her

Hispanic roots? "Guatemala will be a healing experience," our friend Ellen predicted. Settling at the kitchen table, I started dreaming about my own future. The freshly painted and renovated house would soon sell, I could retire and move to Seattle, and thereafter I could engage in my child's life from a respectable distance. I toasted myself and the muggy summer day with a cool beer.

Ten days later Maria was back home.

She had developed a kidney stone from those calcium pills she took religiously without the benefit of fluids because she didn't care for water and there was no soda to be had. The excruciating pain of passing a stone had landed her in the humble clinic where an American physician happened to preside during a two-week volunteering stint. She lay on a cot for two nights with fluids and painkillers dripping from a bag attached to a crooked wooden pole. Next to her, a grandmother was dying, a boy lay in a coma, and a baby was wailing while people and flies crowded around. Maria felt better by the time she called from Father Greg's office, but the doctor advised her to go home since he lacked diagnostic tools and wouldn't rule out complications.

And so I went to Dulles Airport to pick her up, once more dumbfounded by the bizarre turn of events. Whoever is in charge of the universe is messing up big time, I complained to Ellen. "You'd better get with the program," she laughed and kept laughing in a fit of helplessness, admitting that she had run out of words of wisdom for this child.

"I want to kill her," I said to my good friend Mary in Boston.

"For having a kidney stone?"

"Yes!"

"We need to talk," she said, concerned.

"Maria couldn't have made that one up," observed the leader of my Latin American parents support group. "Passing a kidney stone is way too painful."

We consulted a urologist who declared the episode a fluke and thought that Maria could safely return to Guatemala. But by then she expressed doubts about the venture. Culture shock was sending some after tremors.

"People are terribly poor," Maria let me know. "Kids have no toys. They use an empty can to play soccer. And, when they get sick, there's no doctor."

She wasn't sure whether she wanted to return. Perhaps she'll stay, she said. "Doing what?" I asked. We discussed the option of attending the nearby community college. "Maybe," she said.

Meanwhile, she resumed her life of being up or out all night and sleeping during the day while I was at work. When the house sold in August and the moving van rolled around to put our stuff into storage, a decision on Guatemala, college, or whatever loomed large. Okay, she'd go to the community college, she said with an air of doing me a favor. When we perused the list of degree options, she latched on to physical therapist, probably because she'd been manipulated by dozens of them in the course of her soccer injuries. The program was very competitive, warned the admissions advisor, requiring a four-point average. She could do it, she said confidently. We moved her into the garret of a lovely Victorian mansion within a stone's throw of the campus, and in September I bid her farewell with the promise of steady checks and once-a-week phone calls.

At work, I was given a rousing retirement party with the type of laudations you shouldn't really hear before your funeral. USIA granted my wish for a few more weeks of temporary duty in Bosnia, where I covered for the press service the country's first democratic elections after years of harrowing civil war.

"As U.S. taxpayers, you should be proud of your stellar support of Bosnia's slow and painful peace process and the healing of its war wounds," I wrote to friends. "When I arrived in Sarajevo, I felt like I was eight again, walking among the ruins of Berlin. But, looking closely, I see determined efforts to rebuild and to recover. The most visible expressions of this energy and optimism are the little street cafés at every corner—just a bunch of plastic tables and chairs propped against gutted buildings, ready to serve beer, Coke, and tiny cups of Turkish coffee."

My assignment ended with consultations in a few other countries of the former Yugoslavia. The landscapes invited memories of my mother who had been born in the Batschka, a German enclave in Yugoslavia.

My mother was fourteen and in confirmation class when she met my father, her teacher and ten years her senior. He scolded her for being late and promptly fell in love with her. At the time, he was on an internship for the Methodist ministry. They married when she was twenty and served their first congregation in Budapest, Hungary, where my oldest sister Beate was born. By the time I came along, there was an established ritual of summer vacations in the Batschka, the virtual paradise of our childhood.

While Nazi Germany declared war on all fronts and diets became lean up north, we relished Grandma's abundance of foods, including stuffed peppers and sweet corn; goulash and paprika chicken; peaches and grapes; and rich, creamy desserts. We crowded into our cousins' beds, and we played endlessly on the premises of the family business, a lumber mill next to the Danube Canal.

My mother organized the children to put on plays in my grandparents' courtyard. We charged a little admission to keep us flush with *dinars* for the ice cream man. During one memorable performance of *Hansel and Gretel,* my sister Heidi, who played Gretel, threatened to quit unless Beate, cast as the witch, stopped knocking her about beyond the requirements of the script.

Caught up in the minor sibling rivalries, we were oblivious to the encroaching hostility that threatened the good life in the Batschka.

When the war's debacle became apparent and more and more of Tito's partisans appeared in their backyards, German farmers and entrepreneurs packed their bags, hitched their wagons, and started to walk toward the lands from which their ancestors had migrated 200 years earlier. My relatives were among the endless stream of refugees. The old people, including my grandparents, refused to leave, thinking that the turmoil would soon pass.

We learned about their bitter end in the summer of 1945. We were sitting amidst the rubble of Berlin when my mother received the news of her parents' death in a Yugoslav concentration camp.

According to reports, the new communist rulers in Yugoslavia had rounded up the remaining ethnic Germans and transported them by train in cattle cars to a village south of Novi Sad. Several families were shoved into a room and made to bed down on the bare floor. The village was cordoned off—no one was allowed in or out.

As people died of starvation and typhoid, my grandfather, a lay minister, said prayers over the mass graves. After he died, my grandmother, in her black kerchief, continued the prayers until she, too, died. There are no tombstones marking the cruel end of these stranded Germans. Plows have leveled the land.

As part of a personal pilgrimage, I had hoped to visit the Batshka at the end of my Balkan tour. I wanted to pay my respects to golden childhood memories and kind grandparents who had vanished without a trace. But my hopes were soon dashed because, under Slobodan Milosevic, Yugoslavia refused to issue visas to U.S. citizens. There was no point in waiting around, and, after three months in Europe, it was time to go back home and resume parenting.

Maria and I hadn't had much luck connecting. We had agreed that I'd call on Mondays to wake her up at eight, but whenever I dialed from Sarajevo, Zagreb, Ljubljana, or Skopje, I had to leave messages on the answering machine. Concerned, I talked to Maria's landlady, a soccer mom and acquaintance from the time our girls had played in elementary school. "I think she's still attending college," she said. "But since I don't allow boyfriends overnight, Maria is staying out a lot."

That wasn't very reassuring. When I finally caught up with Maria, the report was mixed. She liked her art course, enjoyed math, but had dropped English and psychology. She had been invited to exhibit her art at the downtown YMCA, but didn't make it to the opening because she was in a bus accident that traumatized her previously injured knee. However, she had a serious and cute Moroccan boyfriend. I wasn't impressed.

After returning to DC, I left a few more messages on the answering machine and talked to Maria's landlady, who hinted that Maria was living with said boyfriend and "might even be married by now."

"What?" I cried.

When Maria finally called, I skipped niceties.

"Are you married?" I demanded.

"We need to talk," she said evasively.

"Well, are you married?"

"We need to sit down and have a serious talk," Maria kept insisting and then, caving in, admitted, "Yes, I'm married."

Hanging up, I collapsed into hysterical laughter and just couldn't stop laughing. Tears streamed down my cheeks. Jack, Jane, and eight-year-old Arthur, my hosts, gathered around, wondering whether I had lost it. "She married the Moroccan," I gasped. "Oh, no," groaned Jane. "Congratulations," added Jack. And that mixed review characterized just about everyone's reaction as I spread the news among friends at home and family abroad.

Some, like Ellen, already knew.

She had stumbled upon Maria's secret accidentally. Maria was minding Ellen's dog and cats one weekend, and, when Ellen returned, she took a call from a man who asked for Maria. "Who is calling?" asked Ellen. "Her husband," the man said, and Ellen slammed the receiver down. Driving Maria home, Ellen mentioned the crazy phone call. "He said he was your husband," Ellen laughed. "So you know," Maria said quietly. "What?" screamed Ellen, almost hitting a tree. Bringing the car to a screeching halt, she demanded full disclosure. Meekly, Maria filled her in.

No one of our circle of devoted friends had been invited to witness the October ceremony at city hall in Alexandria, Virginia. "It takes only twenty minutes to get hitched," Maria reported of the event. She wore her silky prom dress, and grainy night photos showed her surrounded by a group of young Middle Eastern men, one of them, Si-Mohammed, Simo for short, my new son-in-law.

I met Maria at church on Sunday where she appeared in a way-too-short miniskirt and made the rounds falling into outstretched arms, including her mom's. Afterwards, we met friends for lunch and an exhibit at the National Museum of Women in the Arts. Maria, exuding a new mature happiness and poise, let us admire her golden wedding band. "I love being married," she confessed with a pride that hinted at superiority. She had, after all, attained a status that had eluded her mother for lack of trying.

We made plans to meet with Simo, who was working as a waiter, but then I came down with a high fever and went to bed with the flu. By the time I recovered, it was Thanksgiving, and our good friend Marian pulled out her dining room table for a dozen guests, including our enlarged family.

I met Simo for the first time at the Falls Church Metro Station on our way to the Thanksgiving feast. He was a short, curly-haired nineteen-year-old with an olive complexion, sprouting adolescent pimples. He had a firm handshake and looked me in the eyes as he extended a bouquet of red roses, wishing me "Happy Thanksgiving." I was instantly impressed with his friendly and self-assured demeanor and heard Maria exhale with relief. Bad press had obviously preceded our first encounter, as Simo later confirmed. "Meeting you wasn't as bad as I expected," he told me.

Sitting at the table, Marian asked us to summarize gratitude in a few words before digging in. Maria said, "acceptance, family, and friends." Simo praised "marriage," and I almost gave thanks for the Moroccan solution, expecting marriage to liberate me from parental crisis management.

After the meal, Simo talked freely about his life and background. Both his parents were dentists, practicing in Casablanca, he said. He had a fifteen-year-old sister and a ten-year-old brother. His family had a beach house. He had grown up surfing and had competed internationally in South Africa and Spain. During high school, he was an exchange student in the United States, and, after finishing school in Morocco, he went to Paris to earn a diploma as a dental technician. Thereafter, he worked in his parents' practice, surfing on weekends. "I'm a beach bum," he explained. Hoping to surf in California and Hawaii, he applied for a U.S. visa through the newly instituted lottery system. He drew a lucky number and won his green card, he said. He had hoped to work as a dental technician but discovered that he needed a U.S. diploma. Meanwhile, he was living hand to mouth working as a waiter.

"Whatever possessed you to get married at nineteen?" I asked.

"Well, I think living this American adventure will be easier with a wife, rather than a roommate," he explained.

"And where do you see yourself in, let's say, ten years?"

"That's impossible to know," Simo said angrily.

Oh yes, I thought, he's grown up in a culture where all plans are *inshallah*—God willing.

At present, he was sharing an apartment with a Moroccan friend, and Maria had practically moved in with them.

Moving again

They were saving for the down payment for their own apartment, and since it didn't make sense for me to continue paying for Maria's room, we loaded her stuff once more onto a rented truck to place it into storage. During the move, I admired Simo's hands-on practicality and enjoyed the kids' playful interactions. At the storage facility, Maria climbed onto the loaded trolley that Simo pushed at top speed along the labyrinth of corridors, taking in a few extra spins. Laughing and screeching at the tricky corners, they finally halted at the designated cubicle. The security camera was beaming their lighthearted romp into the office where the secretary and I watched with amusement. Take-out lunch was on me, and Simo kept inquiring if my coffee had enough cream and if the bagel was as fresh as could be. Everything was just fine, I assured him. And, by the way, what would he like to call me, Valerie or Mom? "I'll call you Mom," he said promptly. Thereafter, it seemed that every other sentence was, "Thank you, Mom," and, "We really appreciate this, Mom," with Maria soon echoing her husband's gracious manners.

"I'd like to serve you a real fine meal at my restaurant, Mom," Simo suggested.

"But you'd have to pay," I reasoned, "And you don't have much money and are saving to get your own place."

"You put me to shame," he said sadly.

When I told Jack of Simo's offer, he admonished me, "You should go. Dress up and order a small entree and no wine, because that's the expensive part. And for dessert have a cup of coffee." And so I turned up in a black dress at Simo's French bistro in Bethesda where the owner and all the uniformed Middle Eastern waiters knew who I was, and Simo hovered over me with courtesies fit for a queen.

To honor the newlyweds, I invited our friends to a reception on a Sunday afternoon, planning to leave for the West Coast the following week. The Warners offered their home for the party, and I decorated a Costco cheesecake, Maria's favorite, with the couple's initials and a giant yin-yang symbol. Maria was excited over the prospect of introducing Simo into our friendly circle and went clothes shopping to look her very best. It would be a belated wedding party for the couple and a farewell for me.

And then, on Sunday morning at 3:30, the telephone rang. Marian, my hostess, handed me the receiver. "It's Maria, she says it's important."

"I'm at the hospital in Arlington with appendicitis, Mom," she said calmly. "I'll be operated on as soon as the surgeon gets here. They are afraid the appendix may have burst. But don't worry. I'll be okay. It's very important to me that you go ahead with the party. Simo will be there."

When I arrived at the hospital, Maria was on intravenous drip, and Simo, who had been up all night, was sleeping slumped over in a chair next to her bed. I took him home to get some sleep and then returned for the operation at ten. I held Maria's hand as she was wheeled into the operating room and talked to the surgeon afterwards. The removal had been clean, he said, and she would be fine and out within a couple of days. After retrieving my cake and hors d'oeuvres from Marian's fridge, I arrived at the reception minutes before the first guests.

A group photo shows our good friends smiling brightly after having recovered from the shock over Maria's most recent misadventure. Simo, who arrived late with his roommate in tow, is sitting in the middle of the front row with both thumbs up. He exudes the self-confidence of a teenager who's made it. Meanwhile, his bride was recovering from anesthesia and, reaching for her wedding band, discovered that it had been stolen.

When I next visited her, a dozen roses from Simo were sitting on the nightstand. Roses, as we learned, were Simo's response to any crisis. He hadn't thought of bringing her toothbrush, nightie, or slippers. Sandra, who lived nearby, took Maria on a slow recovery walk to the hospital store to shop for those essentials. Maria was still in pain and seemed sullen, especially when I broached the subject of insurance and who would pay for the hospitalization. Since her marriage, she was no longer covered under my plan.

"Don't worry," Maria advised. "Simo called Casablanca, and his mom will take care of the bill."

"She's prepared to take care of a $10,000 bill?" I gasped.

"Don't worry," Maria reiterated with a mind-your-own-business undertone.

"Get into that car and start driving," Sandra advised when I expressed my exasperation. And so I packed up and stopped once more at the kids' place in Alexandria where the announcement of my impending visit had unleashed a cleaning frenzy the night before. Maria had directed the vacuuming and dishwashing from her mat on the floor and now sat with Simo at the little round table, the only set of furniture in the living room. I brought an album of Thanksgiving photos with extras for the new Casablanca in-laws.

Maria had been in great pain the night before, Simo reported. She had lost weight and looked pale and wan. How could I leave her like that, I wondered? How could I leave these two kids with no education, lousy jobs, and no health insurance?

"I feel badly driving off," I said bursting into tears. "I feel as if I have failed you. I don't know what to do." Maria put an arm around me and patted me on the back. "I'll be fine. You just go ahead," she said softly.

It was as if our roles were being reversed, and I was the child in need of assurance. It reminded me of another time when she had taken on the role of adult. She was eleven, and we were living in Austria. We were returning to Vienna from a ski vacation near Salzburg. It was February, late evening, and the highway was clouded in thick fog from the nearby Danube. Visibility was less than ten feet, and as I crawled along, cars were zooming by at top speed. They honked angrily as they overtook us, cutting back into our lane within inches. I had seen photos of accidents on that foggy highway, with dozens of cars piled on top of each other, and I was deadly afraid. Pulling into a rest stop, I cried, "I can't drive in this fog. We'll end up getting killed." "Yes, you can drive," Maria said in soothing tones. "Just take a few deep breaths. You can do it." Following her mature advice, I got us home safely.

I've always wondered how our relationship and life would have evolved had I been less the all-knowing, in-charge, fix-it mom. I paid the bills on time, found the right schools and therapists, took her to Costa Rica when she wanted to learn Spanish, and to Weight Watchers when she felt fat. Even when she pushed me to the brink, I knew how to ask for help or dial 911. Rarely did Maria see me despairing, and when she did, she was too preoccupied with her own rages and defiance to notice or care. But during our farewell from life in Washington, she became my consoling little mother who kept patting my back as I sniffled into my hanky. She dismissed me lightly and let me drive off into the sunset toward Seattle, my new home.

15.

LETTING GO

We saw each other only once in the course of Maria's last years, but our roller-coaster relationship continued despite the distance of 3,000 miles.

In my absence, our faithful DC friends rallied around. They gathered for Maria's birthdays, helped her move to yet another apartment, provided references, and set out to find her when she disappeared.

During her first months of marriage, Maria impressed me with a new maturity and mellowness that culminated in the biggest birthday card Hallmark could provide. She topped off their sentimental message with a handwritten note that made me teary. "I now understand that life is hard and making ends meet is very hard. I miss you a lot and am now seeing how hard you worked to get me to do the right things."

We talked at length on Sundays. Her confident and cheerful updates, though belying the reality of her tough life, made me bounce all week. I was relieved to know that Maria was in almost daily contact with Dolores, her mentor from the rites of passage year. Dolores coached Maria how to get a job as hostess at Citronelle, a five-star restaurant in Georgetown, where she presided on high heels in a starched and ironed uniform. When they needed a busboy and Simo was once more out of work, he joined her, though reluctantly. "It's great working together," Maria reported. "In the morning I get him out of bed by kissing him all over. At work I just love seeing his little butt buzz by."

For Mother's Day, I received a package of promotional Citronelle brochures, intended to impress me with Maria's new status. I really got excited when Maria mentioned health benefits after three months at Citronelle, but by then she had quit serving the high life. Her uniform had mysteriously disappeared, and she had been accused of losing the key to the wine cellar, plus botching up some important reservations. Simo, who considered it beneath him to haul dirty dishes, had already quit and was now waiting tables in an upscale Italian restaurant.

Their phone was often disconnected, and Maria kept losing her cell phone. After I didn't hear from her for a month, I asked our good friend Sandra to investigate. "I met Simo at the door of his Italian restaurant," she reported. "'Hi, Sandra,' he called cheerfully, walking toward me as if he owned the place." Sandra got the scoop on Maria who, with help from Dolores, had just gotten a job at Godiva Chocolates. Maria liked to be in touch when life was good, and disappeared from my radar when she felt a failure. Luckily, she kept in touch with Dolores, her faithful cheerleader. "Maria handles marriage in an amazingly mature way," Dolores told me over the phone. But the kids also needed some financial help to move into their own apartment, she suggested.

"Could we borrow $300, Mom?" Maria inquired in her next phone call. They'd borrow another $300 from Simo's parents for the down payment of an apartment, she said. "And I'll pay you back in monthly installments," she promised.

I sent her the check, although I had just finished reading the book *Grown-up Children Who Won't Grow Up* by Larry Stockman, who preached the art of letting go. I had also joined a Seattle parenting group based on tough love principles and was glared down when I reported on my loan in the next session. "You're addicted to rescuing her," observed one parent. "She'll never pay you back," predicted another. I quit the group, thinking that I knew better, but a year later forgave the debt after receiving only one $40 check.

The kids acquired a one-bedroom apartment in a high-rise and quickly accumulated the essentials for housekeeping. Dolores left me a telephone message raving about my child's competent hosting of a dinner party. The table they'd salvaged from next to the dumpster had been covered with linens from Nancy and Sam and china from Marian. Maria served artichokes with dip for appetizer, pasta with veggies as main course, and fruit salad with ice cream for dessert. Two guests sat on a sagging couch, two on wooden crates. "Maria talks about you with affection. You can be proud of her," Dolores concluded. The subtext of this observation was Maria's frequent remark, "My mother didn't raise me to put up with this shit," whenever the conversation strayed to husband Simo.

As phone calls resumed, Maria projected a high spirit with occasional cracks over marital fault lines and cultural clashes. Simo, who got off past midnight, was often met by Moroccan buddies urging him to spend the tips from his lucrative evenings on booze and the boys. Maria would stay up for hours waiting for her husband. "I now know what you went through waiting for me all night, Mom," she confided in a mellow moment. I ached for her. Simo sometimes stayed away for days, insisting that this was his manly prerogative. The lease was in Maria's name, and, every time the first of the month rolled around, she counted nickels and dimes racing toward the deadline. Sometimes they lived on oatmeal, she said.

When their first anniversary approached in October, I asked my married sisters to send messages of encouragement. "Marriage gets better by the year," wrote my sister Heidi who had just celebrated her golden anniversary. "I don't think I'll last that long," sighed Maria. She had a pile of presents for Simo, who—true to style—came through with a dozen red roses. They went out for dinner and dancing and sent me photos of their picture-perfect outing.

We talked for months about my upcoming two-week visit over Thanksgiving, and Maria begged me to stay with them at least for a few days. But then, two days before my arrival, she disinvited me with sobs. "You'd better not come, Mom. The place looks a mess and Simo refuses to help me clean up. He hasn't been home in days, and I don't know where he is." "I'll come anyway," I assured her.

She greeted me barefoot, sweaty, and in shorts, waving a white rag like a city under siege. Her hug was as sticky as the floor. Welcome to life in squalor, I thought, as I surveyed the apartment. On the coffee table was an assortment of cleaning aids and utensils, together with a Costco-special of pink roses. Maria handed me a note from Simo, "I'll see you after work at midnight, Mom!" "He's trying to suck up to you," grumbled Maria, who hadn't seen him in days.

Though it was near midnight, we got down to work. We piled debris and garbage into one corner and dirty laundry into another; we scoured dusty and grimy surfaces, washed the pile of dishes in the sink, and cleaned out the fridge. Maria, now my willing partner, had few homemaking skills. Growing up, she had stubbornly refused to learn, teaching me to pick battles over more important things.

"What's that?" I asked pointing to a brown mark on the living room wall. It looked like someone had thrown a cup of coffee.

"I don't know," Maria shrugged vaguely.

The bathroom took the prize. The clogged bathtub was half filled with dirty water and displayed a history of black rings. Short curls and long black hair covered the sink, bottles of grooming and beautification aids ruled the floor, and the toilet needed more than a brush.

I started emptying the tub with a bucket to get at the drain, clogged beyond Drano solutions. I was Ajaxing when Simo made his exuberant entrance. "Just in time," I said. "You can wash the kitchen floor." Obediently, he changed into shorts and began scrubbing on hands and knees. The kitten in the corner was amazed. It had been one of Simo's impulse acquisitions, brought home with the assumption that Maria would take care of it. The kitten soon became a victim of marital warfare. Its dish was filthy, and the litter box stank to high heaven.

"Cats are very clean animals, but you have to give them a chance to practice their habits," I lectured.

"Yes, Mom," Simo said meekly, cleaning out the poop.

By three in the morning, Maria and I stretched out on the futon with clean sheets while Simo curled up on the sofa in the living room. The apartment sparkled, the pink roses looked perky, and the cat was purring.

I stayed with Maria and Simo for three days and did my motherly thing of driving them to work in my rental car, shopping for household essentials, putting food into the fridge, and cooking a meal. On Sunday, while Simo was working, I gave Maria the choice of a movie or a walk through Christmassy Alexandria.

"Whatever you like, whatever makes you happy," she said. I thought I was dreaming.

"Pinch me!" I said. She did.

"Ouch," I cried.

"You asked for it," she grinned.

We opted for a walk and stopped at a bookstore where Maria headed for the religion section. She wanted an English-language Koran, "So I can better understand where Simo is coming from." It was Ramadan, and Simo spent lots of time with his friends at the mosque, or so he said.

We found a copy and Maria checked the glossary for references to divorce. The Koran gives men the option to divorce if the wife is unfaithful or a bed-wetter, we learned. We couldn't find directives for wives with unfaithful or irresponsible husbands.

That night, Maria curled up with her husband and the Koran on the couch, and Simo read to her page after page in a monotone that put her to sleep. It was time for me to move on.

Our good friend Marian roasted a turkey for an intimate, candle-lit Thanksgiving dinner. Afterwards, I walked arm in arm with Maria and Simo through the dark and desolate suburban neighborhood, singing, laughing, and skipping along. I held on tightly to each child, trying to mend fragile relations.

A mellow Thanksgiving

On my last Sunday, Simo spontaneously suggested cooking a Moroccan supper. He raced to the store and then fired up the stove to prepare a three-course meal. He had learned to cook as a boy helping his mother in the kitchen. At his home in Casablanca, meals were a big midday affair for the whole family, including uncles and grandparents, Simo explained, as he served a variety of tasty dishes we ate using fingers. I asked him to say a blessing, and he recited a string of verses in the guttural sounds of his mother tongue.

As we parted, the kids were full of ambitious plans. Come January, Maria was going to enroll in a college course at Northern Virginia Community College, where we had spent a morning exploring options and assistance for her learning handicap. Her previous attempt at college had ended with the appendectomy.

Simo said that he had to go home to see his mother before her sinus operation. "I've just got to see you," she had been lamenting over the phone. Maria commented, "I don't know where he'll get the money to go. And before he leaves, he'd better give me half a month's rent or a girlfriend will move in and then he can see where he'll stay when he returns."

Like many women of her generation, my daughter was torn between feminine concern and feminist uprising. She set Simo's alarm clock in the morning and called from work to get him going; she worried about his clean shirts and creased pants, and she loved saying "my husband." On the other hand, she wouldn't ever want to live in patriarchal Morocco, she said. "If he leaves and has visa trouble coming back, he'd better not badger me to fix it. And, by the way, Mom," she continued, "he doesn't have a green card."

"But he told me last Thanksgiving how he got it," I countered.

"I told him to lie because you had warned me that he might marry me just to get his residency."

I was speechless.

As it turned out, Simo stayed, and, when they received my Christmas check, Maria went to get a tree and asked Simo to help decorate. "At first he wasn't interested," Maria reported, "but then he got into it. He didn't hang the ornaments in the right places, but you know what? It didn't matter. It just didn't matter." I was pleased that she continued family traditions.

For Maria's twentieth birthday, Don and Sandra organized a dinner party with our friends at Simo's latest restaurant. It was a rousing success and lasted past midnight. Simo was most solicitous to the table of nine and got his fellow waiters to join in the "Happy Birthday" chorus. Maria opened my package and was especially pleased with my big check.

My gift helped them finance their next move to an apartment in the boonies with tennis courts and three swimming pools, but far from public transportation. They bought a car from a friend of a friend, but, after towing it twice from the beltway, decided to junk it. The reason for the big move, I later learned, was to escape Simo's notorious friends. They had gotten him into deep trouble. A woman, who had hung out with the gang, accused Simo of kidnapping and forced sodomy. Maria, the loyal wife, got a $3,000 loan to hire a Moroccan-American lawyer and dutifully went to Simo's arraignment.

In the meantime, she had quit the chocolate store, started at a dry-cleaner's, quit that, and became an apprentice at Domino's. Pizzas would be her big ticket to the future, she told me breathlessly the next time we talked. "My manager is a real cool guy who makes $60,000 a year and thinks that I can make that much within two years. There's a guy who started at twenty, and, within six years, he had his own franchise and made enough money to buy his mom a house." I was all for her making lots of money and buying me a house.

The next time I called, Simo answered and said that Maria was working too late now to make it home via public transportation and was therefore staying with her "twin brother." *Who can that be?* I wondered. Next time I called, I got Simo again with Maria at large. He confessed to marital problems.

"I'm trying to talk to her but she won't listen," he complained. "We all make mistakes sometimes, and I've already changed so much because of her. I give her all my earnings and I come home after work every night. I really want to spend the rest of my life with her." I had little to say, except that he should take good care of himself and not do anything foolish. "Yes, Mom," he promised.

When I hadn't heard from Maria for almost a month, I asked Sandra again to investigate. She soon e-mailed: "Maria looks very well but things are a mess. She hasn't been in touch with you or those of us here because we didn't think it was a good idea to get married so young, and now it hasn't worked out well. Simo sent her flowers Monday and I guess would like to be back with her but offers nothing to bring that about, like getting a job or getting away from his ne'er-do-well friends, one of whom was asleep on the apartment living room floor when Maria went over yesterday to collect some things. And there was dope in the apartment, and, if the police raid it, she will be arrested, since the apartment is in her name and she will not be able to start the management program on May 1. She is to move to a Falls Church Domino's in a week or so. She is at Gary's but not sleeping with him.

"No, do not pick up the phone and call her. Hang on, Valerie. She is okay. Honest. And sorting through this."

I followed Sandra's advice, and, whenever my anxieties overwhelmed me, I put Maria into the light. When I saw her surrounded by radiance, she looked self-confident, relaxed, full of purpose, and cheerful. But would my mental exercises make a difference in her life? "Yes, she'll feel it," said my Quaker friend Mary.

Maria finally called me past midnight on Mother's Day. She cried for an hour. It was as if she had saved up all her grief and tears just for me on this special day. I listened. She needed to get away from Simo and his friends, she said. He had been harassing her with dozens of daily phone calls, had sent roses and threats through his friends, who appeared regularly at the pizza store. One night, when she was alone and in charge of closing, Simo's friends arrived to tell her that Simo was lying in wait for her. He would kill her unless she returned to him, they warned. In a panic, she called her former boss, who came to pick her up in his car. She had contacted the police for a restraining order, but, since she couldn't provide Simo's latest address, the police could not do much for her. She needed a car to feel safer and to get around, she cried. Without a car the whole management internship was in jeopardy.

I decided to give her money for a good used car and consulted with our friend Jack Warner who had been very successful with his own used-car purchases. "Five thousand would get her a pretty good Toyota," Jack advised. "Give her another thousand for new tires and the insurance and she should be set." Jack started marking up *The Washington Post's* classifieds while I wired Maria the money with the advice to get in touch with Jack. My child was mellow and grateful.

She was also full of hope and exciting news. At work, she had met John, who "treats me like a queen." Pending the sale of John's trailer home, they planned to move to Ocala, Florida, where John's parents lived. Meanwhile, they were working long hours delivering pizza, Maria in her newly purchased VW, bought at an auction. "Thank you so much for the money, Mom." No, she never got in touch with Jack Warner; she took care of the purchase herself. True to pattern, the clunker soon broke down, needing a new motor. "Could you wire me another $3,000, Mom? I'll be sure to pay you back," she pleaded. No, I couldn't, I said, and there followed a few more weeks of non-communication until my friends informed me of Maria's farewell party.

They staged it at a restaurant and also invited John, "so he can see that Maria is loved and appreciated by a family of friends," as Nancy and Sam put it. Maria's new man, Marian reported, was a clean-cut, twenty-eight-year-old army veteran with an Asian background and some skills as a car mechanic. He was the unmarried father of two children, and my friend Lois coaxed some baby pictures out of him. He seemed a bit inflexible, "But maybe that's what Maria needs at this moment," said Sandra. Sam, the professor, conducted a long interview and found out, among other things, that John's mother rode a Harley Davidson. "Do you have a large family?" Sam asked. "Not like this," John responded, glancing around the table. "I think he was impressed," said Jane.

"You can be proud of your daughter," said Lois, describing how Maria went around the table in the course of the evening, engaging everyone in charming conversation. She was looking forward to living in a warmer climate, she said. She was sick of Simo and his friends and needed a new start.

At the beginning of November, Maria called our friends announcing her departure. "She still has most of that Maria exuberance," Sandra e-mailed. "It sounds like it has taken some hits, though."

When Maria finally called me from Florida around Thanksgiving, she cried mostly. She and John lived in a trailer in northern rural Florida with bare cupboards but plenty of roaches. They had worked for a while unloading trucks for K-mart, but then were laid off. She went back to Domino's for minimum wage and had to walk for an hour for lack of public transportation. As she trudged along the highway, she worried about her debts, which had turned astronomical because she had missed monthly payments. "Simo, the jerk, who is the reason for the first loan, doesn't pay a dime, and I have no idea where he is," she sobbed.

John, the "man who treats me like a queen," turned out to be no prince. By Christmas he had acquired a new girlfriend, and Maria had to witness nightly goings-on through paper-thin walls. He was also fighting extradition to Tennessee and prison for non-payment of child support.

In my Christmas letter to friends, I wrote, "I have not seen Maria in over a year and have been without an address and phone number for her for most of the time. Our good friends in DC gave her a farewell, and pictures show my dark-haired child with blond streaks. I am very glad that she has contacted me from Florida, and we now talk at least once a week. At the end of January, she will turn twenty-one. No, she doesn't want me to visit her, and no, she cannot come to Seattle because she has to get her life together before she sees me again, she says. I am surrounded by her excellent framed art on my walls and think that her talents and superior IQ should lead to more than baking pizza and loading trucks. But what do I know? I'm just a mom. When Maria was fifteen, she once belted from the pulpit at our All Souls Unitarian Church Kahlil Gibran's poem 'Your children are not your children ... You may give them your love but not your thoughts, for they have their own thoughts.' My daughter continues to teach me some difficult lessons."

For Maria's twenty-first birthday at the end of January, Sandra invited our friends to a party, and, one by one they talked to Maria on the phone, giving her lots of advice but also assuring her of their enduring love. She followed up on one suggestion by filling out forms for the divorce, leaving a blank for her husband's address. Simo surprised me one day with his cheerful, "Hi, Mom, how are things in Seattle?" He had moved to Miami, he reported, was surfing during the day and waiting on tables at night. He wanted to get in touch with Maria, and I promised to let her know.

"He is in Florida? And I tried to get away from him!" she shrieked. As soon as she got in touch, he started bombarding her again with phone calls, even getting members of his family to call, urging reconciliation. Occasionally, he sent small checks with the advice, "Enjoy yourself." She wavered between rage and ambivalence toward him, and the divorce forms remained incomplete, also because he refused to let her know his whereabouts. He pursued her relentlessly until the end. During our last phone conversation before her death, Maria warned me that her number would be disconnected again because Simo had tracked her down and was resuming his harassment.

By then, Maria felt assured of David's love and the goodwill of his whole family. In August, she had moved into David's little house on his parents' property and those last weeks were the happiest of her young adult life.

The six previous months had been a nightmare of homelessness and shortstop jobs. For a while, she slept on the living room couch of a Carlos, then settled on the couch of some Joe. She moved furniture for Closet Maid, waited on tables in a restaurant, and stocked merchandise in the Dollar Store. She walked for miles to and from work, was always short on money, and had no bank account for fear of her creditors. She desperately needed a car, she said, and was saving for one.

"I'll match your savings," I offered.

"Could I send you my paychecks and you save them for me, Mom?" she asked.

"Sure," I said.

For a moment, I had forgotten those years when I had deposited her savings into an account, only to be asked soon afterwards to retrieve the cash. Anger usually accompanied these transactions, and now I was afraid of repeating the pattern. When I consulted our friend Ellen, she advised, "Stay out of Maria's financial mess. She'll have to do both—pay her debts and save. It will be her only way to get control." Another friend suggested that Maria get in touch with a local credit service for free and confidential counseling. Over the phone I found a woman in Ocala who was ready to help. When I informed Maria that I had changed my mind and suggested consulting the credit service, she doused me with fury.

"You're like someone who puts a bone before a hungry dog and then takes it away. I can't ever trust you, and I'm tired of your asinine advice!"

I apologized and admitted that my thinking was often muddled.

"Don't ever fucking call me again," she raged and then the line went dead.

"Put her in the light," advised my friend Penny, who had raised six children. "I'm sure she'll contact you again."

Luckily, I had a live report on Maria from my sister Claudia that spring. She and husband Dick visited Maria in Ocala and found her cheerful, looking well and healthy. "Stop worrying," my sister admonished with three exclamation marks. "Remember, Maria is a survivor!"

In June, Maria sent two screaming letters spiked with f-words. "I am moving shortly," she hinted mysteriously. "If you want a relationship, write back."

"Yes, I would like to have a relationship with you," I wrote back promptly. "But I don't want to be your punching bag. When I read your angry letters, I feel hurt, crummy, sad, awful. Hope to hear from you. Love, Mom"

I found my card among Maria's few belongings after her death.

"She told me about your difficult relationship," Natasha said at the funeral in Florida. "She kept saying, 'I'm finished with kicking the dog.'"

"What did she mean?" I asked, not familiar with the expression.

"I think she realized that she had to stop blaming others and take responsibility for her own actions. 'I'm finished with kicking the dog,' she kept saying. You know, Maria really loved you."

16.

PUZZLES

I met Natasha and David Rahme for the first time in front of their sprawling red farmhouse in Silver Springs, Florida. Sobs and silence had interrupted our phone conversations since the accident, as we discussed coffins and a funeral, the cruel details of death's demands on the living. Nothing but kindness toward me had shone through their parental grief. *Of all the people in the world, they know how I feel*, I thought, as my sister Claudia and I walked with outstretched hands toward David and Natasha.

They led us to the little bungalow where David and Maria had lived. A bucket and broom leaned against an outside wall, reminders of Maria's recent attempts at housekeeping. Inside, some of her stuffed animals sat on a windowsill next to the tiny blue Colombian *zapatos* she had worn on arrival in America. Ripped jeans and designer sweats were spread over the bed.

"I went through these because the undertaker asked for clothes," Natasha explained. "He thinks he can fix the injuries well enough for a viewing. I think I'll give him this," she said, holding up a white, two-piece dress with lovely embroidery down the front.

"I let Maria borrow the dress for a wedding she and David recently attended. Maria just loved it and looked great. 'Nan, if I'm real careful, can I borrow it again?' she asked." Natasha carefully draped the dress over her arm. Maria would also be buried with the beaded earrings and little pouch David's dad had made for her. The pouch was yellow, blue, and red—the colors of the Colombian flag. Maria had been a little vague about their sequence, "So I went to the library to look them up," David's dad explained.

As we left the bungalow, he pointed to the air-conditioner his son had fixed just a few days before. "He was very good at electrical stuff," he said. "Had been trained in the army."

Little by little, I learned more about the handsome young man, whom Maria called "the love of my life."

He was seven days old when Natasha took him into her arms and made him the charming center of their family. He was the son of David's half-sister, who traveled with a circus and seemed to thrive on casual encounters. "I've got a baby and intend to give him up," she informed Natasha one day over the phone. "Do you want that baby?"

"Do we want that baby?" a stunned Natasha asked David at his office.

"No," he said without hesitation. They had just finished raising Natasha's two sons from a previous marriage and had done enough parenting, he reasoned. Not convinced, Natasha consulted her sister Nocker.

"Do you want that baby? Of course you want that baby," Nocker admonished. "You feed dogs and cats. You can feed a baby."

And so Natasha flew to Hartford, Connecticut, and received the infant wrapped in a blanket, his formula in a brown bag. They named him David after his adoptive father. He grew up tall and athletic, with blue eyes and blond curls, a warm heart, and a winning smile. He made friends easily, and, if someone needed a meal or a roof over his head, David brought him home to mom and dad, who had taught him to be generous.

When Maria met David over billiards, he was almost twenty-two and in limbo. During the summer months he had worked as a lifeguard in a fancy resort, often finding himself at the center of a gaggle of giggling girls vying for his attention. Lately, he had joined a construction crew. "David worked only when he needed money," his father explained with a twinge of disapproval. The relationship with their son had its wrinkles, especially when David took in stray friends who got him to drink too much. "Sama and Dragon (David's nickname) drunk as shit," Maria noted in her daily planner. "Dragon's mom really mad."

According to the police report, David had been legally drunk at the time of the accident. Natasha contested that, pointing out that David was taller and heavier than noted in the report; considering his actual height and weight, his alcohol level was below the legal limit, she argued. The urine analysis of the young man who sat in the back of the car showed substance abuse. Maria had no traces of alcohol or illegal drugs, and she was the only one who was wearing a seat belt. She died from blunt force as the car hit a pine tree at sixty miles per hour. She died almost instantly.

A woman who lived near the crash dialed 911 and ran toward the car. She called out to the occupants, but there was silence except for David's groans.

He outlived the others by about an hour. "I think Maria finally came to take him with her," said his father. "I imagine that she said, 'Okay, David, time to go.'"

They knew Maria as a strong partner, one who put direction into the relationship. In the short time the Rahmes had known her, they had loved her dearly, I realized, as they pointed to Maria's favorite places in their home.

She'd sit right there on the floor in the country kitchen, tutoring their wayward nephew in math. And this was her favorite chair for curling up with the cat while the dog craned his neck for attention. Natasha had caught the scene on film, one of the many photos she had taken of Maria's new life with David, to be sent to Mom in Seattle. Now the pictures were spread out on the kitchen table, giving me a glimpse of a life that had been.

"And here's the puzzle we had been working on," Natasha said, lifting the cloth over a thousand pieces on a card table. "Maria was so good at it— found the pieces real quick and got the picture going." The puzzle's frame was firmly established; the center, still a gaping hole. "I guess we'll have to finish it without her," Natasha said, replacing the cloth.

Maria left more puzzles than the one on the card table, as it turned out.

There was her family composite, to begin with. Her parents hadn't gotten along and split, she had told her new friends. Her mom lived in Seattle; her dad was still in Colombia. She had an older sister, Rosa, a very talented artist who lived in Baltimore. But Rosa had gotten into drugs and then disappeared. And she had a twin brother, Emilliano, who had died a year ago from a heart attack. He was a doctor.

"A doctor at twenty? How can that be?" asked Natasha.

"He was just brilliant," came the answer. "I miss him terribly."

Natasha and David were amazed when I filled them in on the facts.

"And I kept thinking we've just lost one child but this poor woman has lost two within one year," David exclaimed. There was no twin, I told the Rahmes. Or was there?

In a box of Maria's few belongings, I discovered a black-and-white-speckled notebook dedicated to Emilliano Chapa, 1/24/79–8/13/99, "to my best friend, heart, soul, other half, twin." The entries are full of passion and longing for her twin. "To my best friend in life and death. I love you and miss you so much. I live with you in my mind forever. I will try to make you proud. Parted twins will always find each other to complete one soul, someone told me. We will be together one day and I will be able to tell you face-to-face. I love you more than anything."

The entries span about a year, from the time Maria left Simo to the time she met David. Who was this Emilliano, the recipient of inconsolable grief, desperate entreaties, remorse, pain, helplessness, and hopelessness? Racking my brain, I vaguely remember Maria telling me about a new Hispanic friend in the DC area who had suddenly died of a heart attack. On the phone, Maria had seemed upset while I offered a lame, "I'm so sorry you lost a dear new friend so suddenly." Had this friend provided the blueprint for Emilliano, her "twin?" Simo knew about the twin brother, and so did Maria's co-workers. "Now she is reunited with her twin," said Claire, a young woman Maria had befriended at Domino's.

The notebook took my breath away. Claudia, who was the first to read it after we retired to our motel room, shook her head and said, "I think she was schizoid."

"Nonsense," said my friend Lorin, a psychotherapist. "Maria obviously had a desperate need for a confidante and wrote to this Emilliano. If she hadn't, she might have gotten into drugs."

What stunned me was the depth of Maria's despair. According to the notebook, John, the "man who treats me like a queen," was distant and indifferent. He was critical of her, used her at night but left her feeling worthless at daybreak.

"I am some short, chubby Latino girl that is not very pretty, don't have great anything, and I am so lost," she writes. "I know I am not very pretty, don't have a great body, don't have a lot going for me. Each day I wonder who I look like, Mom or Dad."

"I would give almost anything to talk to you," she tells Emilliano. "Sometimes I look at the star and wish you could see me. I wonder how you are. Will you still care if no one else does? I am so alone."

Maria never let on how miserable she really was during her trailer months with John. "Last week we had a really good long talk," she'd tell me, adding, "Time will tell whether we'll stay together." She had been invited to his uncle's house for Thanksgiving, she reported, but wasn't sure whether she'd go. For one thing, she didn't have a thing to wear. "How about that short, pleated black skirt with a white blouse?" I'd suggested. Okay, she'd wash and iron the blouse, she agreed.

In the diary she tells Emilliano that she had a good time at the feast, talking to many nice people. However, I am dismissed. "John is lucky he has his mother, father, friend and kids," she writes. "I have my Valerie when it is convenient. That is almost never. To her I am always doing the wrong thing, and nothing I ever do will ever be right. In conclusion, I am all alone. I have no one. It used not to matter when I had you, but my whole world is falling apart without you. I want so bad to shut down. I feel like never talking to anyone ever gain. Sometimes I am so lonely without you, I wish I could die. Help!" And in another entry: "I feel like my whole world is crashing right in front of my face. I feel so hopeless, tired, scared, lost, confused."

She was also in physical pain from the old soccer injury that affected her knee. She had no health insurance and no money to consult a doctor. "I don't know what to do," Maria tells Emilliano. "I am trying to keep my world together. I am so sick, and I feel like I want to die. My legs hurt so bad. Sometimes they hurt so bad, I wish I could pass out. Right now I am hurting with this cold and legs, and I am so scared that if I slow down, I will fall apart. I miss you."

What was I to make of this notebook, I asked the therapist I sought out several months later. I put the black-and-white-speckled diary into her hands, hoping for insight and oracle pronouncements. "This book was not written for you," she pointed out, making me realize that I certainly wouldn't want my mother and family to read the secret lamentations I've poured into diaries since I was twelve. Perhaps Maria should have taken the book to her grave and spared me the biggest shock after her death. But I was a mom who wanted to know the crevices of her child's heart. Wasn't I entitled? "There was a time when I knew everything about her—what she ate and what she pooped, what made her happy and how to fix her problems," I cried. "And then I became clueless." Yes, that's the way it was, nodded my therapist, making sure I had enough tissues for my tears.

As for the notebook's content, she explained: "Maria did not have time to integrate her feelings and experiences. You also don't know what her life would have been like without you. She could have died at the orphanage or in Colombia's civil war.

"Maria had mixed feelings about you. She tested you for years and years, expecting that you would reject her so she would have proof that she was shit. She felt a terrible conflict within herself and projected it onto you. You do know that there was love, but you also felt her hatred. Would there have been healing? We don't know because Maria lacked continuum."

This made sense. Still, there was the mystery of Emilliano, the twin. Did Maria perhaps have a twin, or an early memory of a twin?

According to scientific studies, "twin-ness" is ingrained on the brain in utero. "We know that the fetus has an active mind," explained a woman friend who retrieved through counseling her earliest memories of a twin brother. "Growing in my mother's womb, I had an awareness that there was someone, and I felt a closeness that can't be replicated anywhere else. Throughout my life, I've had problems with closeness because I've always been looking for my twin.

"As a child," my friend recalled, "I always had an invisible playmate, an invisible twin who provided a comforting presence." Maria likely had a living twin, my friend suggested. Perhaps she was separated from him as a toddler, abandoned by a mother who couldn't take care of two. And, although Maria's awareness of her twin brother had lain dormant through part of her life, it surfaced during her period of greatest need.

In this life, we'll never know. A verse from the Christian Bible, chiseled onto Maria and David's shared gravestone, sums up our earthly bewilderment: "For now we see through a glass, darkly; but then face to face: Now I know in part; but then shall I know even as also I am known. (1 Corinthians 13:12, King James Version)

Maria was happy during the last three months of her life, Natasha kept telling me. "She was so in love, and I know that she and David were meant for each other. I believe they already had plans for a winter wedding out on our lawn." I couldn't hear enough about my happy girl, and begged David and Natasha to fill me in on all the details, especially those hours before her death.

Maria in Florida

On the evening of November 15, 2000, David's dad made a pot of spaghetti. "The one thing I can make that I knew David liked," as he said.

They ate as a family, and Maria especially loved Natasha's garlic bread. "Teach me how to make that, Nan," she begged.

"There's more to cooking than garlic bread, Maria Consuelo Kreutzer Mendez Benkarani," David teased good-naturedly.

"I know," she admitted. "I don't really know what you see in me, especially with all these pretty beach girls around you."

"But I love *you*, Maria," he said, hugging her.

Then their dog took off with one of Maria's stuffed animals, and, barefoot, she raced after it, fussing and giggling.

There were plans for the next day. Maria would use Natasha's car to drive to her new job at the hardware store and come back for lunch. David and his dad planned to stop at their favorite coffee shop on the way to David's construction site. At around 9:00 p.m., David and Maria took Natasha's blue Buick to drive Wayne, a young man, home. He and his pet snake had been staying with David and Maria for a few days. The snake had been caged, but would get out every so often and scare Maria half to death. The guys grinned at her shrieks.

The night was clear as the three traveled north on the well-marked County Road 314. A few feet from the Dream-Catcher Farm, a thirty-miles-per-hour sign warned of a sharp curve to the left. That's where the Buick veered off the asphalt and slid along the sandy embankment, crashing into a pine tree.

Why did David hit the curve at high speed and then lose control? his parents kept asking. David was a reliable and experienced driver, and he wasn't really drunk, Natasha argued. Maybe David tried to avoid hitting an animal—brown bears had been sighted in the area's woods. Maybe another car drove them off the road. Perhaps David was distracted by an affectionate Maria? And what about that snake? It wasn't in the terrarium at the house when they came looking. It must have been in the car and perhaps it got lose and frightened Maria and made David lose control. "I think it was the snake," Natasha told the investigating officer. "But where is it?" he kept asking.

About four weeks after the accident, a very nervous young woman approached Natasha in the grocery store.

"I know who you are," she whispered. "I know something about the accident. But I can't talk about it. Just want you to know that it wasn't your son's fault."

"Please, please come with me to the police," Natasha pleaded.

"No, I can't. They'd kill me," the woman said.

"But I'll help you; I'll give you money to get away," Natasha cried, now down on her knees.

"No, I can't; they'll find me," said the woman and disappeared.

In the end, the pine tree was our only witness. It had been badly injured, and its wound looked life threatening. We leaned against its trunk and cried while listening to the whispers of its branches. "This tree is not your enemy," said Ellen who accompanied me on a visit six months later. "The tree is your friend. It absorbed the violence of the accident and set your children free." By then the wound was healing. "How do you do it?" I asked the tree. "Nature taught me," it said.

Over the years, the healing tree has become a symbol for my own journey of recovery. After I had become a practitioner of meditation, an image of oneness with the pine inspired a poem.

I AM THE TREE

"I am a tree," suggests my meditation master,
As I search through images that flood the mind,
Until I see it:
My tree,
The tree,
Rooted in Florida's sandy soil,
Tall, strong, and slender,
With contoured bark and needled branches,
Guarding the deadly curve of a rural road,
Helpless against the screeching and careening car
That flings my child and two companions
With sixty-miles-an-hour speed.

The onslaught shakes me to my roots
And scars me with a gaping wound.
Trembling, I shield the groans of children dying,
I, the tree, the only witness to their passing.

Freed, she dances higher, higher,
Circles, hugs my crown and whispers:
"You must stay rooted,
Until you, too, are free to dance some day."

Losing a child leaves a hole in your heart, and the search for wholeness is lifelong. Mine took me to Thailand where I learned to meditate at a Buddhist monastery and to Mexico where I observed *dia de los muertos* [day of the dead] rituals. What I learned in Mexico, I bring back to November visits in Florida when I meet the Rahme family at our children's grave. We usually start by cleaning the site, and then spread our blankets for a picnic. We remember our children with favorite foods, with laughter and some tears. And, when we walk away, we have the feeling that Maria and David would have liked the party.

Sometimes we recite a Native American poem David's dad discovered at a flea market.

I AM NOT HERE

Don't stand by my grave and weep
For I'm not there, I do not sleep.
I am a thousand winds that blow,
I am the diamond's glint on snow,
I am the sunlight on ripened grain,
I am the gentle autumn's rain.

When you awaken in the morning's hush,
I am the swift uplifting rush
Of quiet birds in circle flight,
I am the soft stars that shine at night.
Do not stand by my grave and cry,
I am not there, I did not die.

In my vertical house in Seattle, the third-floor bedroom offers a view of the Cascade Mountains. During the winter, sunrises are especially brilliant as the whole sky explodes in deep red, golden yellow, and eggplant purple. Whenever I admire the spectacle, I secretly think that Maria, my artist, painted the sky—just for me.

Her presence is often tangible. Like when I burrow my face in the teddy bear she left on my dresser. As I inhale, I'm back bending over her forehead with a kiss that sends her off to school.

During the months of sleepwalking unreality after her death, I once returned with groceries from the Safeway and had a vision of Maria huddling with her Colombian clan.

"Come," she motioned, opening the circle. As I approached, I noticed that her people were shorter than mine. Linking arms, I had to bend a little, wanting to belong.

EPILOGUE

Maria's story is intertwined with my own story of remembrance, loss, and healing. Like the tree that absorbed the fatal car crash and survived with a scar, I've also been marked for life. And like the tree that continues to thrive, I have recovered with a renewed sense of *joie de vivre*.

To honor Maria's legacy, family and friends have created scholarships at Chelsea School in Silver Spring, Maryland, and at Solebury School in New Hope, Pennsylvania. Royalties from the sale of this book will be donated to the Maria Consuelo Funds at these two schools.

CPSIA information can be obtained
at www.ICGtesting.com
Printed in the USA
FSOW02n1546041016
25732FS

9 780595 497058